this book belongs to:

....

SASHA
in good taste

SASHA
in good taste

Recipes for Bites, Feasts, Sips & Celebrations

SASHA PIETERSE

photography by
ELIZABETH MESSINA

FOR MY LOVING HUSBAND, HUDSON

*Babe, you have supported every dream
I've ever had. No matter how big or small,
you are always there to help make my
dreams a reality. No one loves me the way
you do. I promise to spend every day of my
life making sure I support and love you
the same way. Thank you for being
you: my consistent and incomparable
partner in this life. I love you with
all my heart and soul.*

CONTENTS

WELCOME
NOTE

For as long as I can remember, I have loved entertaining. Whether it be on the big screen or in my own home, I get so much joy out of making others feel welcome.

I was born in Johannesburg, South Africa, to wonderful parents who instilled in me an incredible love of food and travel at a young age. My parents were professional dancers specializing in adagio (fancy lifts and tricks) and performed in our hometown and all over the world. When we were home, we'd indulge in many of South Africa's yummy delights, including one of my favorite desserts, *melktert*, a Dutch cake that's been making hearts happy since the sixteenth century. My *ouma* is famous for her *melktert*, and I definitely got my sweet tooth from her. And I can't forget all the savory dishes, meat pies, sausage rolls, biltong (South Africa's version of beef jerky) . . . I could go on forever!

But my love for food didn't stop in South Africa. Before I turned three, we found ourselves in Nice, France, where I discovered a deep appreciation for croissants and decadent French pastries. In the year that we lived in Nice, it's safe to say my cheeks got a little rounder and a little rosier. I can still remember the beautiful beaches, the friendly lady at the local market, and the many cute cafés along the way. It was a pretty spectacular life for a toddler!

Not long after Nice we emigrated to the USA, leaving our family and friends behind to start a new journey. Ironically, my food journey was not as progressive as my new life. I became a very picky eater, much to my mother's despair. While I turned my nose up at the cuisine I had once loved, I discovered, like many, the allure of acting in La La Land. My love for entertaining—something that came so naturally to me—really blossomed when I starred in my first TV show, *Family Affair*, in 2002. From that point on, I knew I wanted to entertain people for the rest of my life, and that love of acting and entertaining helped me rediscover my deep love for food and expand my palate with new meals and experiences.

Time jump! In 2009 I started filming the first season of *Pretty Little Liars* and my time on camera coincided with changing my entire outlook on food. Long workdays inspired me to make yummy and health-conscious choices of food that wouldn't bore me and would give me lots of needed energy. Working in Hollywood has its benefits but also its downsides,

should take what we put in our bodies seriously. The more comfortable I got in the kitchen, the more I loved it and wanted to experiment.

Fast-forward: When Hudson and I bought our first home, a whole new world opened up for us. It was so exciting to have a house of our own, and even better, we finally had a space to share with others. Since then our house has seen a lot of action, whether it's dinner for four or Friendsgiving for eighty. From annual Halloween parties, Thanksgivings, and Christmases to summer block parties, "paint and wine" soirées, and more, we have truly done it all and enjoyed every minute of it.

For us, whether it's breakfast, lunch, dinner, or the bites in between, it's always a family affair (including the family you choose). It's a time when we take a break from our chaotic lives to laugh and lean on each other. Papa, my grandfather on my mother's side, cooked for the entire family almost entirely by taste and I am positive that's what he passed down to me. It's way more challenging for me to calculate and measure every morsel . . . but don't worry, I did *just for you*.

It can be *a lot* to cook and host, but I make sure to find the balance between throwing the "perfect" party and truly being in the moment. You can

especially when it comes to body image. It was and still is very important to me to take care of myself in a way that doesn't harm me in the long run. Thanks to a few mentors, including a very sweet little lady who now happens to be my mother-in-law, I learned the importance of fresh food and why we accomplish *both*! I have found where my passions meet my personal life, and it's hosting. Hudson describes the time before guests arrive as my "magic hour," because no matter how much still needs to be done, it always comes together. I've learned how to prioritize and plan but, more important, I've learned how to relax and let go. Through many exciting years of trial and error, I've learned the real dos and don'ts of hosting and I am so excited to share them with you.

Perhaps my favorite part of cooking and baking and mixing is relishing the way it brings my friends and family together. Food instantly creates a sense of comfort and connects people in a way that is unexplainable but simply undeniable.

My hope is that through *Sasha in Good Taste* you will find the inspiration and confidence to throw your own celebrations, big or small, and thoroughly enjoy them. This book is filled with crowd-pleasing, beginner-friendly, and impressive recipes that will make your party planning easy and stress-free. Hosting can seem intimidating and sometimes unattainable, but here you will find all of the tools you need to effortlessly execute the party of your dreams. Thank you for joining me as I take you through my party prepping process and what feeds my soul.

Welcome to my home.

Love, Sasha

HOW TO USE THIS BOOK

There's a lot of love infused into these pages, but there's also a lot of practicality to go along with it. Part of what makes party planning fun and successful is being able to use your imagination. The same rules apply for making yummy food. But with cooking and baking comes a list of instructions, and the way you follow them can make or break your dish (and your appetite). I've added these notes to start you out on the right track!

HOW TO READ A RECIPE

That sounds silly, right? Reading a recipe doesn't sound complicated at all, but not reading it carefully is the most common mistake some folks make!

STEP 1: Read the recipe, and then read it again.

STEP 2: Make notes! The more I make a dish the more I figure out what works best. Write your own notes so that you remember what worked best for you for next time.

STEP 3: Double-check that you have enough time to make the recipe.

STEP 4: Make sure you have all of the ingredients listed.

STEP 5: Clean and prep your space.

STEP 6: Follow the recipe step by step.

RECIPES

I've always felt that cookbooks should be guides and inspiration givers, not rulebooks. Sure, there are certain instructions that you should follow such as oven temperatures and measurements, but I highly recommend you get creative with my recipes to suit your taste buds and the preferences of your special guests.

PARTY TIME

The same rules apply for my party guides. My favorite part of throwing parties is making them feel personal and really stand out. My tips and tools on party prep and design will show you how easy it is to customize parties to your lifestyle and interests. Whether you're throwing a party for yourself, a family holiday gathering, a special occasion with a special someone, or just because . . . there are plenty of amazing designs and themes that you can easily create yourself.

MY RECIPES AND PARTIES ARE geared toward being simple but effective. Anyone can make these dishes and drinks and cater to their party guest list. Cheers to lots of happy tummies and smiling faces!

DO YOU HAVE IT?

In my own cooking, I make sure all the ingredients I use are organic and as nutritious as possible, so even though I don't specify that in my "whatcha need" lists, I definitely recommend trying to buy the healthiest and highest quality ingredients available. Here are the items that are always in my pantry and in my refrigerator.

FOR COOKING:

OILS:
Coconut oil, grapeseed oil, olive oil, truffle oil

LIQUIDS AND DRESSINGS:
Balsamic reduction or glaze, lemon juice

HERBS AND SPICES:
Basil, dill weed, mustard seeds, oregano, pepper, pink Himalayan sea salt, red pepper flakes, rosemary, thyme

OTHER:
Almonds (sliced) and crackers that are worthy of a cheese platter, such as thin wafers or some delicious artisanal Italian crackers

PERISHABLES:
Butter (unsalted), Brie, goat cheese, garlic (fresh), lemons, limes

FOR BAKING:

DRY INGREDIENTS:
All-purpose flour (unbleached), gluten-free flour, baking soda, aluminum-free baking powder, unsweetened cocoa powder

SWEETENERS:
Brown sugar, cane sugar, powdered sugar, honey, maple syrup

SPICES:
Cinnamon (ground), cinnamon sticks, cloves (ground), nutmeg

COLORS AND FLAVORS:
Almond extract, vanilla extract, natural food coloring

OTHER:
Chocolate chips, white chocolate chips

PERISHABLES:
Butter (unsalted), eggs, buttermilk, whole milk, heavy cream

FORGOT IT?

Don't sweat it! Here are some easy ingredient replacements.

1 tsp baking powder =
¼ tsp baking soda + ½ tsp cream of tartar

1 tsp baking soda = 4 tsp baking powder

Butter = coconut oil or unsweetened applesauce
(for baking purposes only)

1 cup buttermilk = 1 cup plain yogurt

¼ cup cocoa powder =
1 oz melted unsweetened chocolate

1 tsp cream of tartar =
2 tsp lemon juice or vinegar

1 egg = ¼ cup unsweetened applesauce or
¼ cup banana (for baking purposes only)

1 cup evaporated milk = 1 cup light cream

1 tsp lemon juice = 1 tsp white wine

1 tsp lime juice = 1 tsp vinegar

1 cup sour cream = 1 cup plain yogurt

TOOLS
AND TIPS

Here are some cooking essentials for my recipes!

ELECTRIC TOOLS:

Food processor
Hand mixer
Stand mixer

ESSENTIAL TOOLS:

Baking pans, round (small, medium, and large)
Baking sheets
Bread knife
Cheese grater
Cheese knife
Chef's knife
Cooling racks
Cutting board
Icing knife (offset spatula)
Mixing bowls
Muffin tins (mini and regular)
Oven mitts
Paring knife
Pots (small, medium, and large)
Rolling pins
Saucepans (small, medium, and large)
Scissors
Silicone spatulas
Skillets
Tongs

DISPOSABLE ESSENTIALS:

Foil
Parchment paper

CLEANING ESSENTIALS:

Make sure you have a good, nontoxic kitchen counter cleaner and sanitary sponges. Bleach and other harsh chemicals and products can harm you and your furry family members, too. It's always a good idea to check the labels on all of your cleaning products. Remember to clean as you go, not just for convenience but for safety, too, whether it's rinsing out bowls or wiping down countertops.

CONVERSIONS

Temperature and measurement conversions are a lifesaver if you're limited on tools or livin' life in a different country.

TEMPERATURE:

250°F = 130°C	400°F = 200°C
275°F = 140°C	425°F = 220°C
300°F = 150°C	450°F = 230°C
325°F = 165°C	475°F = 245°C
350°F = 175°C	500°F = 260°C
375°F = 190°C	

MEASUREMENTS:

Measurements are rounded.
1 ounce = 30 grams
2 ounces = 56 grams
3 ounces = 85 grams
4 ounces = 115 grams = ¼ pound
8 ounces = 225 grams = ½ pound
12 ounces = 375 grams = ¾ pound
16 ounces = 454 grams = 1 pound
32 ounces = 907 grams = 2 pounds
1 kilogram = 1,000 grams = 2¼ pounds
1 teaspoon = ⅓ tablespoon =
    5 milliliters
1 tablespoon = 3 teaspoons =
    ½ fluid ounce
2 tablespoons = 6 teaspoons =
    ⅛ cup = 1 fluid ounce
4 tablespoons = ¼ cup
5 tablespoons + 1 teaspoon = ⅓ cup
8 tablespoons = ½ cup = 4 fluid ounces
10 tablespoons + 2 teaspoons = ⅔ cup
12 tablespoons = ¾ cup

16 tablespoons = 1 cup = 8 fluid ounces =
    ½ pint

32 tablespoons = 2 cups = 1 pint

4 cups = 32 ounces = 2 pints = 1 quart =
    1 liter

4 quarts = 1 gallon = 128 fluid ounces =
    3.78 liters

HOW TO HOLD A KNIFE

8-INCH CHEF'S KNIFE

You will use this knife for nearly every meal. When you hold it, it should feel comfortable, like an extension of your own arm. This knife is mainly used for dicing and chopping. With your dominant hand, pinch the knife blade between your thumb and pointer finger just above the handle. Now grip the handle with your other fingers. With your other hand, hold the ingredient you're cutting with your fingers curled into a "C" shape or "claw" to prevent any loss of digits. Remember to cut with the entire blade, working in a steady rocking motion.

PARING KNIFE

A paring knife is made for peeling and trimming; it's also great for scoring meats and making teeny tiny slices or cutting an avocado! Paring knives are used for more detailed work, and in places where you want direct control of the blade. Hold your paring knife the same way you would a butter knife, then adjust your thumb and index finger by moving them just above the handle, resting them against the dull sides of the blade; this should feel comfortable enough so that you can use the whole blade in one motion. Hold the food vertically with your index finger on the top and your thumb on the bottom.

When trimming produce, remember to cut carefully in a downward motion toward your thumb. Make sure you hold this knife, or any knife, with clean dry hands to avoid any accidents.

BREAD KNIFE

Self-explanatory—this one is for cutting bread. However, the serrated blade of this knife is also good for slicing tomatoes and other produce with thin skin. A solid, sturdy grip on the handle of a bread knife is all you need.

HOW TO SLICE IT

DIFFERENT CUTS:

SLICE: cut into long strips

DICE: cut into small cubes resembling dice

CHOP: make medium-small cuts of produce

MINCE: chop produce finely using a rocking motion

OBLIQUE: also known as the roll cut; cut from side to side to create pieces of food with two angled sides

JULIENNE: cut into thin short strips

BIAS SLICE: cut at a 45-degree angle to produce elongated oval slices

CHIFFONADE: for large-leaf herbs—stack a few leaves together, roll them, and slice to create ribbons

BRUNOISE: very finely dice produce

SUPRÊME: remove the peel, pith, and seeds from citrus segments

TRIM: cut off the ends of produce, meat, or poultry

Our food is affected by the "Big Bad 6": preservatives, pesticides, processed foods, chemicals, additives, and politics.

Unfortunately, it's rare that we truly know what's going into our food nowadays. If you read a food label and the ingredients are unfamiliar and sound scary, there's a good chance they are. A lot of our regular food items are filled with things our bodies don't appreciate. Some of the most common dietary misunderstandings come from these labeling terms: low-fat, nonfat, trans fat–free, sugar-free, and guilt-free. We are constantly being told that dairy, gluten, fats, and sugar are bad for us. Well, that's not always the case; it's how the food has been modified, added to, and messed with that's truly harming us, and future generations of eaters. I believe it's vital and potentially lifesaving to know what we are putting into our one-in-a-lifetime bodies. The road to being health-conscious starts with understanding ingredients lists and making the right choices.

Politics come into play when we get down to the price tags. The government departments that are in place to keep our foods safe have had their hands tied, and the result is that our health is at risk. Here are a few statistics to help you understand how serious this issue is and how we can make better choices:

- 14,000 man-made chemical additives enhance the shelf appeal of our food.
- In the United States alone, it is estimated that we consume an average of 1 billion pounds of chemical additives a year. That is approximately 6 to 9 pounds per person per year.
- These chemicals, additives, preservatives, sweeteners, and so on are widely believed to be the cause of many diseases and conditions like behavioral disorders, hyperactivity in children, growth stunting, unexplained weight gain, heart disease, cancer, high blood pressure, seizures, mental health disorders, serious food allergies, kidney and liver failure, asthma, strokes, and rapid aging.

I want to give you a quick cheat sheet, so you can recognize the no-nos on your next trip to the grocery store, and then I promise we'll get back to the fun stuff. (Though there's no better way to enjoy a life of fun than to keep your body healthy and happy!)

SWEETEN-NOS AND OTHER "FLAVORS"

ASPARTAME

Aspartame is one of my least favorite of the artificial sweeteners since people with diabetes and those who have hormone disorders (like me) are often encouraged to turn to sugar-free sweeteners, sugar-free gum, and foods and drinks containing aspartame. It's most commonly used in diet drinks, gum, mints, candy, and other sweetened products. Aspartame has been a controversial ingredient for years, but somehow we still have it on our shelves and in our sweetener packets at our local coffee shops. Some known side effects include mood disturbances, seizures, cancer, and more.

HIGH FRUCTOSE CORN SYRUP

If you've never been told that high fructose corn syrup is bad for you then you may be living under a rock. But have you ever been told *why*? It's a sweetener made from corn and it's popular with manufacturers because it's cheap, sweet, and maintains its freshness and moisture for a suspiciously long time. The bad news is it's known to cause accelerated aging, raise cholesterol levels, and contribute to heart disease, making you more susceptible to blood clots. Yikes.

MSG

Also known as monosodium glutamate, hydrolyzed soy protein, or autolyzed yeast, MSG is made up of naturally occurring components in our bodies of water. However that doesn't mean it's okay to be ingested. It's used as a flavor enhancer in seasonings, condiments, chips, and more. It's also known to cause seizures, burning sensations in the chest and forearms, chest pain, and nausea.

BIOCHEMICALS AND PRESERVATIVES

BHA

Also known as butylated hydroxyanisole, BHA is a preservative found in many of our favorite foods and drinks including, but not limited to, beer, butter, cereals, boxed dessert mixes, and gum. To put it simply, the National Institutes of Health categorizes it as a "human carcinogen." No thanks.

SODIUM CASEINATE

Sodium caseinate is a biochemical that's used in many dairy products and is known to cause dairy intolerances. Large quantities of this chemical can

also harm your kidneys and lead to other reactions including respiratory arrest.

CANOLA OIL

You may be surprised to see this on the list since canola oil is advertised as one of the healthiest oils on the market. When the rapeseed plant (used to make canola oil) was genetically modified it became a phenomenon in the world of agriculture because of its ability to withstand drought. However, the oil from the seeds of the plant contains high amounts of erucic acid, a fatty acid connected to heart damage, particularly Keshan disease. Canola oil is also known for causing calcification and inflammation of the arteries. It's also known to be unsafe for infants and can cause stunted growth.

OF COURSE, ALL THE CHEMICALS and additives I listed can be hard to avoid since they are present in so many of the food items we typically use.

I know it's almost impossible to stay away from all of these ingredients, but I do the best I can! Here are some good labels to look for when shopping:

Preservative-Free
Non-GMO
No MSG
100% Organic
No Artificial Flavors
No Artificial Colors
No Aspartame
Made with Coconut Oil
Sweetened with Honey or Maple Syrup
Sprouted Grains
Cage-Free/Free-Range
Grass-Fed
Locally Grown

Remember that just because a product's label looks pretty and claims it's healthy doesn't mean it is. Always read your ingredients lists to double-check. Becoming your own expert is empowering and important!

HEALTHY ALTERNATIVES

SWEETENERS

Cane sugar is a better alternative to most sugar-free options—ONLY because of how terrible sugar-free options are. If you're looking for good sugar alternatives, organic honey (especially straight from the comb) or pure maple syrup (with nothing else added) are so delicious. They're also easy for your system to digest. *(If you have diabetes or are sensitive to sugar, check with your doctor before trying anything new.)*

DAIRY

Dairy lover? It's always better to get whole milk, or full-fat dairy items. I know it goes against what most of us have been taught to buy, but the truth is . . . if you're going to have dairy you want the closest to natural as possible. Look at those ingredients lists!

OILS

When you are cooking at a temperature that's 420°F or higher you should always use a high-heat oil. Olive oil will burn with high heat and will leave you with a bad taste in your mouth, quite literally. When olive oil reaches this state it also loses many of its health benefits. When cooking at a higher temperature than normal I like to use coconut oil, sunflower oil, or grapeseed oil. All three are high-heat oils that won't burn or change flavor when cooking. Okay, let's eat!

SAVORY

JALAPEÑO BITES

If peaches are out of season, these bites will still taste delicious without them.

MAKES 24 BITES | PREP TIME: 25 MINUTES

whatcha need

High-heat oil or butter, for the muffin tin

1 (16-ounce) package phyllo dough, thawed but cold

16 ounces Brie, cut into ½-inch slices

4 ounces spicy jam or pepper jelly

2 ripe peaches, thinly sliced

2 jalapeño peppers, thinly sliced

Balsamic reduction, for drizzling

tools required

Mini muffin tin, 2½-inch round cookie or biscuit cutter (water glass works, too), paring knife, cheese knife or butter knife

whatcha gotta do

Preheat the oven to 400°F. Make sure your phyllo dough is completely thawed but a little colder than room temperature. With a high-heat oil or butter, grease 24 cups of a mini muffin tin so it's ready to go.

On a clean flat surface, unfold the phyllo dough. Phyllo dough is naturally flaky, so don't worry if the dough sheds a little bit. With a 2½-inch round cutter, cut rounds of dough and gently press them into the cups of the muffin tin allowing for some pleats around the edges. Bake until the phyllo cups reach a light golden brown, 10 to 15 minutes.

Remove the phyllo cups from the oven (leave the oven on) and stuff each cup with a cube of Brie, a spoonful of pepper jelly, a peach slice, and top it all off with a jalapeño slice. Return to the oven and bake until you see the bites bubbling, another 2 to 5 minutes. Let the bites cool for a minute, then drizzle with the balsamic reduction and serve.

MELON SKEWERS

If you want to jazz this recipe up, lightly drizzle balsamic reduction over each skewer and sprinkle with coarse sea salt and freshly ground black pepper. They're always a huge hit so be prepared for these guys to go fast!

MAKES 24 SKEWERS | PREP TIME: 25 MINUTES

whatcha need

1 honeydew melon

16 ounces mozzarella cheese, cut into ½- or ¾-inch slices, to taste

1 (16-ounce) package pitted dates

1 (8-ounce) package sliced prosciutto (about 24 slices or 12 slices cut in half)

tools required

Chef's knife, paring knife, cheese knife, toothpicks or mini skewers

whatcha gotta do

With a chef's knife, halve the melon and scoop out the seeds. Cut into thick slices and use a paring knife to cut the melon flesh off the rind. Then cut the slices into 1-inch cubes.

Onto toothpicks or short skewers, thread a melon cube, then a mozzarella slice, a date, a slice of prosciutto, and then another cube of melon.

WATERMELON CAPRESE

whatcha need

1 small watermelon

1 (6- to 8-ounce) package goat cheese

2½ cups fresh basil

1 (4-ounce) container pomegranate seeds

Balsamic reduction, for drizzling

tools required

Chef's knife, paring knife, serving platter

whatcha gotta do

With a chef's knife, slice the watermelon crosswise into 2-inch-thick slices. I tend to measure my slice next to my pinky; there's no need for them to be perfect, just similar. Use a paring knife to cut the melon flesh off the rind, then cut the watermelon slices into 2-inch cubes. Watermelon seeds do not bother me, but you are welcome to keep or remove them based on your preference.

Spread goat cheese onto the side of the watermelon that's facing up. Garnish with a basil leaf and top it off with pomegranate seeds. Place all of the cubes on a serving platter and drizzle with balsamic reduction. Enjoy!

STUFFED JALAPEÑOS

MAKES 12 BITES | PREP TIME: 15 MINUTES

whatcha need

Oil, for baking sheet

6 jalapeño peppers

1 bulb garlic, minced

1 (12-ounce) container cream cheese

1 (6-ounce) package sliced prosciutto

tools required

Bread knife, paring knife, hand mixer with a whisk attachment, baking sheet, mixing bowl

whatcha gotta do

Preheat the oven to 400°F. Grease a baking sheet with oil so it's ready to go.

With a bread knife, halve the jalapeños lengthwise. Gently pull out the "guts" of the jalapeño, separating the seeds from the membranes. Place the seeds in a bowl and discard the membranes. Make sure you keep your now gutted sliced jalapeño shells safe since you will be using these for your base. Add the garlic and cream cheese to the bowl. With a whisk attachment on a hand mixer, whip the garlic, jalapeño seeds, and cream cheese until the seeds and garlic are evenly distributed throughout. Add a spoonful of the garlic cream cheese to each jalapeño half and then wrap up each half with a prosciutto slice. Arrange the wrapped jalapeños on the baking sheet and bake until the cream cheese is bubbling, about 10 minutes. Let cool for a few minutes and then serve.

PRETZELS

whatcha need

1 packet instant yeast (2¼ teaspoons)

1½ cups lukewarm water

1 teaspoon pink Himalayan sea salt

1 tablespoon dark brown sugar

1 tablespoon unsalted butter, at room temperature

3¾ cups all-purpose flour, plus more for the work surface

½ cup baking soda

Coarse salt, for topping

Pretzel Dip (page 31)

tools required

Stand or hand mixer with a dough hook, large spatula, large pot and lid, parchment paper, measuring cups/spoons, chef's knife, 2 baking sheets, mixing bowl

whatcha gotta do

Preheat the oven to 400°F. Line two baking sheets with parchment paper.

In a bowl, mix together the instant yeast and lukewarm water and let sit for a minute. Add the sea salt, brown sugar, and softened butter. With your mixer, begin to slowly mix while adding 3¾ cups flour, 1 cup at a time. Mix the dough until it is fully formed. It's also okay to use your hands! The dough shouldn't be sticky, so add a little extra flour if needed. On a lightly floured flat surface, knead the dough and shape it into a ball. Cover the dough with a paper towel and let it rest for about 10 minutes.

Meanwhile, bring a large pot of water to a boil. Once at a boil, add the baking soda.

Once the dough has rested, use a chef's knife to separate the dough into ⅓-cup portions. Roll each portion of dough into a 20-inch rope. Take both ends of the rope and twist around the tips forming a circle (tied at the top). Bring the tied ends toward the opposite end to form a pretzel shape and lightly press into place. Repeat this process with all of the dough.

With a large spatula, lower a pretzel (one at a time) into the baking soda water. Only submerge the pretzel for 20 to 30 seconds max or it will taste like baking soda— gross. Once the pretzel is out of the water, place it on the lined baking sheet. Repeat the process with all of the pretzels. Sprinkle coarse salt over the pretzels and bake until golden brown, 15 minutes. While the pretzels are baking, make the Pretzel Dip. Let the pretzels cool slightly and serve with the dip.

SAVORY

27

I can-knot wait for you to try these!

PRETZEL DIP

This delicious dip is a perfect pair with my homemade pretzels (page 26).

MAKES ROUGHLY 14 OUNCES OF DIP | PREP TIME: 10 MINUTES

whatcha need

Oil, for the pan

1 (12-ounce) round Brie cheese

½ cup garlic cloves, finely minced

⅓ cup fresh rosemary needles, gently removed from their stems

1 teaspoon dried basil

1 teaspoon dried oregano

1 teaspoon dried parsley

½ teaspoon pink Himalayan sea salt

tools required

Medium saucepan and lid, chef's knife, paring knife, cheese knife, measuring cups/spoons

whatcha gotta do

Coat a medium saucepan with oil. With a cheese knife, cut the rind off the Brie and then cut the Brie into thick slices. Add the cheese and garlic to the saucepan over medium-low heat. Add the rosemary, basil, oregano, parsley, and salt and cover the pan. Stir the sauce occasionally until the cheese has fully melted and the rest of the ingredients are evenly mixed in, 10 to 15 minutes. Your dipping sauce is ready to serve, and if timed correctly, so are your pretzels!

BLACKBERRY LEMON TOAST

MAKES ROUGHLY 6 SLICES | PREP TIME: 25 MINUTES

You will have at least half of a baguette left over after making this recipe, so go to page 56 to see all the fun sammies you can make with your leftover bread.

whatcha need

Grapeseed oil, for drizzling

1 small baguette, thickly sliced

1 (8- to 12-ounce) package goat cheese

1 teaspoon fresh lemon juice

1 (16-ounce) container blackberries (3 to 4 cups)

Balsamic reduction, for drizzling

½ cup fresh mint leaves, for garnish

tools required

Baking sheet, bread knife, 2 mixing bowls, measuring cups/spoons

whatcha gotta do

Preheat the oven to 400°F.

Drizzle oil onto a baking sheet and add the bread slices, spreading them evenly apart. Drizzle the slices with more oil and bake until they are starting to toast, 4 to 5 minutes.

Meanwhile, in a bowl, mix together the goat cheese and lemon juice. In another bowl, lightly smoosh the blackberries with a fork.

Once the bread is done toasting, spread each slice with the goat cheese mixture. Now add a generous amount of smooshed blackberries to each slice. Lightly drizzle balsamic reduction over each slice and garnish with a mint leaf and serve.

WHIPPED RICOTTA CHEESE TOAST

This toast, plus the other three toasts here, are delicious and shareable, so for parties I like to present them on a lazy Susan or a big platter so you can get a bite of all four. You will have at least half of a baguette left over after making this recipe, so go to page 56 to see all the fun sammies you can make with your leftover bread.

whatcha need

Grapeseed oil

1 small baguette, cut into 1-inch-thick angled slices

Freshly ground black pepper

1 (15-ounce) container ricotta cheese

3 garlic cloves, minced

¼ teaspoon pink Himalayan sea salt

3 tablespoons honey

Red pepper flakes

tools required

Baking sheet, bread knife, paring knife, hand mixer, mixing bowls, measuring cups/spoons

whatcha gotta do

Preheat the oven to 400°F. Grease a baking sheet with oil.

Lay the baguette slices evenly on the baking sheet. Drizzle with oil and sprinkle black pepper over each slice. Bake until the toasts brown slightly, 4 to 6 minutes.

Meanwhile, in a bowl, combine the ricotta, garlic, and sea salt and use a hand mixer to whip on medium.

Once the toasts are ready, top each with a dollop of ricotta. Drizzle with honey and sprinkle with red pepper flakes.

SAVORY

AVOCADO TOAST

I adore avocado toast and how easy it is to whip up in the morning or for a quick afternoon snack.

MAKES ROUGHLY 6 SLICES | PREP TIME: 15 MINUTES

whatcha need

Grapeseed oil

1 large loaf soft whole-grain bread, cut into thick slices

Freshly ground black pepper

3 avocados, halved and pitted

2 teaspoons fresh lime juice

¼ teaspoon garlic powder

¼ teaspoon pink Himalayan sea salt

Sprinkle of paprika

Sprinkle of dried thyme

Lime slices, for garnish

Thyme sprigs, for garnish

tools required

Mixing bowl, paring knife, bread knife, baking sheet, measuring spoons

whatcha gotta do

Preheat the oven to 400°F. Grease a baking sheet with oil so it's ready to go.

Drizzle oil over the bread slices and sprinkle pepper onto each slice. Bake until golden brown, 4 to 5 minutes.

Meanwhile, scoop the avocado flesh into a bowl. Add the lime juice, garlic powder, salt, ¼ teaspoon pepper, paprika, and dried thyme. Mix the ingredients until they are evenly distributed.

Once the bread is toasted, spread each slice with the avo mixture and garnish with a lime slice and fresh thyme.

BURRATA-PESTO CROSTINI

MAKES ROUGHLY 6 SLICES | PREP TIME: 25 MINUTES

You will have at least half of a baguette left over after making this recipe, so go to page 56 to see all the fun sammies you can make with your leftover bread.

whatcha need

Grapeseed oil

1 baguette, cut into thick slices

Pink Himalayan sea salt

3 cups Fresh Pesto (recipe follows)

1 (12-ounce) container burrata

2 cups dried cranberries

2 cups fresh basil leaves, for garnish

tools required

Mixing bowl, bread knife, paring knife, baking sheet, measuring cups/ spoons

whatcha gotta do

Preheat the oven to 400°F. Grease a baking sheet with oil.

Drizzle the bread with oil and sprinkle with a little bit of sea salt. Lay the slices evenly apart on the baking sheet. Bake until the bread starts to toast, 4 to 5 minutes.

(In the meanwhile, make your pesto!)

In a bowl, mix together the pesto and burrata with a fork. Once the bread is toasted, add a generous amount of burrata pesto to each slice and garnish with cranberries and a basil leaf.

FRESH PESTO

whatcha need

Olive oil, for the pan

2 cups pine nuts

¾ cup high-quality olive oil

3 cups fresh basil leaves

1½ cups shaved Parmesan cheese

1 cup garlic cloves, whole but peeled

½ teaspoon pink Himalayan sea salt

½ teaspoon freshly ground black pepper

tools required

Food processor, small skillet, measuring cups/spoons

whatcha gotta do

In a skillet, heat a small amount of oil over low heat. Add the pine nuts to the pan and lightly toast—this should only take a minute or two. In a food processor, combine the olive oil, pine nuts, basil, Parmesan, garlic, salt, and pepper and process until smooth.

SUMMER SALAD

whatcha need

8 cups field greens, washed and dried

8 cups arugula, washed and dried

4 ounces Pear Paradise Dressing (recipe follows on page 43)

1½ cups sliced almonds

3 cups strawberries, cut into quarters

2 peaches, sliced thinly

Fresh edible flowers (pansies are my favorite)

tools required

Serving bowl, tongs, paring knife, measuring cups/spoons

whatcha gotta do

In a serving bowl, combine the lettuce and arugula and slowly pour in the dressing. Add the almonds and use your serving tongs to toss the lettuce. Add the fruit and garnish with flowers. Serve!

PEAR PARADISE DRESSING

MAKES 10 OUNCES | PREP TIME: 10 MINUTES

whatcha need

- ¾ cup olive oil
- ¼ cup champagne vinegar
- 3 tablespoons fresh lemon juice
- 3 tablespoons pear juice (unsweetened)
- 3 garlic cloves, minced
- 1 teaspoon cane sugar
- ½ teaspoon freshly ground black pepper
- ¼ teaspoon pink Himalayan sea salt

tools required

Mixing bowl, canning jar or sealed container, whisk, measuring cups/ spoons

whatcha gotta do

In a bowl, whisk together the olive oil, vinegar, lemon juice, pear juice, garlic, sugar, pepper, and salt. Pour into a sealable container and refrigerate until ready to serve. It will keep for up to 7 days.

ADULTING SPAGHETTI

I call this Adulting Spaghetti for good reason. Even though spaghetti is a childhood comfort food (and not at all hard to make), you can "adult" it by giving it an upgrade with truffle oil and pine nuts. Whenever I make this spaghetti I always feel all grown up and confident in my ability even though it's almost as easy as making ramen. Truffle oil brings an abundance of flavor and complements many different proteins and side dishes, so have fun!

MAKES 2 TO 4 SERVINGS | PREP TIME: 20 MINUTES

whatcha need

1 (16-ounce) box spaghetti

3½ tablespoons truffle oil

4 to 6 tablespoons high-quality olive oil, to taste

1 tablespoon unsalted butter

½ cup pine nuts

5 garlic cloves, minced

½ teaspoon freshly ground black pepper

¼ teaspoon pink Himalayan sea salt

Freshly grated Parmesan cheese, for serving

tools required

Large pot, paring knife, colander, measuring cups/spoons

whatcha gotta do

Bring a large pot of water to a boil. Cook the spaghetti according to the package directions. Drain and return the pasta to the pot.

Add the truffle oil, olive oil, and butter to the pot and toss to coat. Once the butter is completely melted, stir in the pine nuts, garlic, pepper, and salt until evenly distributed. Immediately serve with as much fresh Parmesan as you'd like on top.

SASHA'S SCRUMPTIOUS WAFFLES

I love the readiness of packaged waffles that I can just throw together when I'm still sleepy, but if you have the energy to make waffles from scratch, all power to you! If you're feeling ready to take on the world, think about giving your waffles some pizzazz by adding maple extract or food-safe lavender oil to your batter. The waffles'll be unforgettable!

MAKES 6 TO 8 SERVINGS | PREP TIME: 20 MINUTES

whatcha need

Oil, for the skillet

1 (12-ounce) package sausages (I prefer turkey or chicken sausage), cut into ½-inch slices

1 (8-ounce) package nitrate-free bacon, cut into small squares

1 (12.3-ounce) package toaster waffles

2 pears, thinly sliced

Pure maple syrup, for drizzling

tools required

Skillets (large and medium), toaster, paring knife, chef's knife, serving platter

whatcha gotta do

In a medium skillet, heat a little oil over low heat. Add the sausages and keep watch to make sure they're browning evenly. In a large skillet, over medium heat, add the bacon and cook until sizzling and fully cooked to a desired crunch (or lack thereof).

Toast the waffles and arrange them on a serving platter. Scatter the sausages and bacon over the waffles. Top them off with the pear slices and lightly drizzle with maple syrup . . . yum!

tip To make this dish extra special, I like to use a cookie cutter to shape the waffles. I truly believe they taste better that way.

BURRATA MEATBALLS

If mangoes are not in season, you can substitute another fruit glaze or balsamic reduction.

MAKES 6 TO 8 SERVINGS | PREP TIME: 40 MINUTES

whatcha need

TURKEY MEATBALLS:

1 pound ground turkey

1 large brown egg

¼ cup fine dried bread crumbs

5 garlic cloves, minced

2 tablespoons dried oregano

2 tablespoons dried parsley

2 tablespoons freshly ground black pepper

1 tablespoon pink Himalayan sea salt

¼ cup grated Parmesan cheese

2 tablespoons olive oil

1 teaspoon dried rosemary

Oil, for the pan

MANGO SAUCE:

2 mangoes, peeled and cut into small cubes

2½ teaspoons olive oil

2 teaspoons fresh lime juice

1 teaspoon cayenne pepper

½ teaspoon pink Himalayan sea salt

ASSEMBLY:

1 (12-ounce) container burrata

tools required

Large skillet, paring knife, mixing bowl, measuring cups/spoons, food processor or high-powered blender, chef's knife

whatcha gotta do

MAKE THE TURKEY MEATBALLS: In a large bowl, combine the ground turkey, egg, bread crumbs, garlic, oregano, parsley, pepper, salt, Parmesan, oil, and rosemary. With clean hands (gloves are a great option, too), mix the ingredients together until they are evenly distributed.

In a skillet, heat some oil for a few minutes over low heat. Form 1-inch balls and add them to your skillet carefully. Gently move them around every few minutes until they are evenly cooked.

MAKE THE MANGO SAUCE: In a food processor (or blender), combine the mango cubes, ½ cup water, oil, lime juice, cayenne, and salt. Process until completely smooth with no clumps.

TO ASSEMBLE: Arrange the meatballs on a serving platter. Make sure you drain any excess liquid from the burrata and then add to the top of the meatballs. Drizzle the mango sauce over the meatballs and cheese and serve.

VEGGIN' OUT

The usual store-bought premade veggie platters are often sad and lifeless, so cutting your own veggies and mixing your own dip really sets yours apart. This recipe is a perfect work snack and an impressive party plate, too!

PREP TIME: 8 MINUTES FOR THE DIP; VARIES FOR THE VEGGIES DEPENDING ON THE AMOUNT YOU'VE CHOSEN

whatcha need

3 types of veggies (the amount will depend on your party size and container size): large carrots (harvest carrots if in season), cucumbers, baby tomatoes

YUMMY RANCH DIP:

2 cups full-fat sour cream

1½ cups mayonnaise (canola-free)

1 cup buttermilk

3 tablespoons apple cider vinegar

3 garlic cloves, minced

1 tablespoon dried chives

1½ teaspoons dried dillweed

1 teaspoon dried parsley

Dried basil, to taste

Dry mustard, to taste

Freshly ground black pepper, to taste

Garlic powder, to taste

Onion powder, to taste

½ teaspoon dried oregano

½ teaspoon pink Himalayan sea salt

tools required

Serving platter or vases, chef's knife, mixing bowl, measuring cups/spoons, whisk, paring knife, serving bowl

whatcha gotta do

Wash your veggies. Cut the cucumber into sticks or small slices depending on your desired shape. Cut your carrots into 3-inch sticks. Add your veggies to a serving container or a clean, food-safe vase like mine.

MAKE THE YUMMY RANCH DIP: In a bowl, whisk together the sour cream, mayo, buttermilk, vinegar, garlic, chives, dill, parsley, basil, mustard, pepper, garlic powder, onion powder, oregano, and salt. Whisk until dip is smooth and creamy. Transfer to a serving bowl.

CHEESE PLATE

Cheese platters are not only one of the easiest party starters, but also one of the most loved. So how do you make yours a little fancier than the rest?

tip 1 VARIETY: Have a varied selection of cheeses and not just your favorite kind. Some people like the creamier cheeses like Brie and goat cheese, others like stinky cheeses like blue cheese. Successful cheese platters will appeal to everyone's unique taste buds.

tip 2 FULL CREAM: Bottom line, full-cream cheese just tastes better. A good chef can taste the difference and so can your guests.

tip 3 GIMME THE CRACK-ERS: Picking the right bread and crackers makes a world of difference! You want a mixture from soft breads to thin crackers to complement the different cheeses.

whatcha need

An assortment of at least 4 different types of cheese

At least 3 salty and 3 sweet pairings for the cheeses (e.g., Marcona almonds, prosciutto, cornichons, figs, dried mangoes, dark chocolate)

Delicious crackers and fresh bread

Plus, a cute serving platter and cheese knives

SAMMIES

The best part about sammies is that they are a totally stress-free solution to a cooking time crunch (or a tight budget) for a party or gathering. The second-best thing about sammies is that you don't *really* have to do any hard work, you just need to provide the ingredients and your guests will do the rest, and have fun doing it! Creating a gourmet sandwich bar is easy and oh so tasty.

I love to jazz up a regular turkey sandwich with some arugula and spicy pepper jelly with salt and vinegar chips in the middle. Encourage your guests to create their own delicious and crazy combinations, too!

PREP TIME: 15 MINUTES

whatcha need

A SELECTION OF BREAD: **Sourdough, French rolls, brioche, multigrain, gluten-free**

A SELECTION OF PROTEIN: **Turkey, prosciutto, smoked salmon, ham, chicken breast**

A SELECTION OF TOPPINGS: **Red leaf lettuce, romaine, arugula, tomato, sprouts, pickles, apples, cheese, onion, salt and vinegar chips**

A SELECTION OF SAUCES: **Pesto, mayonnaise, pepper jelly, olive tapenade, mustard**

tools required

A large serving platter, serving spoons and knives, name tags for foods if you're worried about allergies

whatcha gotta do

Cut and clean any ingredients as necessary. Arrange the ingredients in the order that you would make a sandwich in, starting with the bread.

GRAZING TABLE

A grazing table is similar to the sammies bar because of its simplicity and effort level. It keeps guests content for the duration of your party and it looks beautiful!

There are so many tasty ways to assemble a glamorous and crowd-pleasing grazing table—here are a few of my favorite options.

whatcha need

FRUITS AND MORE: **Grapes, different types of berries, cherries, figs, clementines, dried fruits such as apricots, dates, olives, French pickles, chiles (e.g., shishito peppers and jalapeños), sun-dried tomatoes, goji berries**

NUTS AND SEEDS: **Pumpkin seeds, almonds, Marcona almonds, cashews, pistachios**

CHEESE: **Brie, goat cheese, blue cheese, Gouda**

CURED MEATS: **Prosciutto, salami**

OTHER: **Crackers, rosemary, honeycomb, jams, jellies, edible flowers**

tools required

Extra-large flat serving platter or cheese board, serving utensils

whatcha gotta do

Arrange your platter so that everything is accessible. I like to keep it color coordinated to really catch the grazer's eye, but anything goes!

SWEET

CHURRO BOWLS

whatcha need

1 stick (4 ounces) unsalted butter, plus more for greasing the mini muffin tin

¼ teaspoon pink Himalayan sea salt

1¼ cups all-purpose flour

2 large brown eggs

⅓ cup sugar

½ tablespoon ground cinnamon

½ teaspoon ground nutmeg

Ice cream (pick your favorite!)

tools required

Mini muffin tin, hand mixer or stand mixer, medium saucepan, mixing bowls, measuring cups/spoons, small bowl, parchment paper

whatcha gotta do

Preheat the oven to 425°F. In a medium saucepan, combine the butter, sea salt, and 1 cup water. Heat over low until the butter is completely melted. Transfer to a bowl (or the bowl of a stand mixer). Slowly mix in the flour and eggs until a dough texture is achieved with no lumps or dry flour residue.

Turn a mini muffin tin upside down and grease the outside of the muffin cups with softened butter. Divide the dough into 1½-inch balls. Mold the dough balls over the inverted muffin cups, using every other one (leaving a cup empty in between). Transfer to the oven and bake until the churro bowls are starting to turn a golden brown, 25 or so minutes.

In a small bowl, mix together the sugar, cinnamon, and nutmeg. Once the churro bowls are baked, gently remove them from the muffin tin and roll them one at a time around in the cinnamon-sugar mixture. Set upside down on parchment paper until ready to fill. You might have to stir the sugar mixture between churro bowls to make sure the sugar doesn't clump together. When all of the churro bowls have had their sugar bath, fill with your favorite ice cream and serve.

GREEK YOGURT PARFAIT

These delicious parfaits are perfect for brunch or a sweet occasion like a bridal shower. They are also a light and healthy dessert option that you don't often see at parties. You can always play with the colors of the yogurt, too: If you're throwing a baby shower, match the yogurt to the baby's gender with some all-natural food coloring; if you're throwing a Fourth of July BBQ, use strawberries, blueberries, and regular Greek yogurt to match the flag. You get the idea, so run with it! When you're serving your parfaits, make sure they stay in a cool and shaded place to preserve their freshness.

MAKES 8 TO 12 PARFAITS, DEPENDING ON SIZE OF SERVING CUPS | PREP TIME: 15 MINUTES

whatcha need

1 (14-ounce) package graham crackers

4 to 5 cups berries, sliced if large (your favorite; I like strawberries)

2 (20-ounce) containers full-fat Greek yogurt

Honey, for drizzling

tools required

Serving cups, chef's knife, large zip-top plastic bag

whatcha gotta do

Place the graham crackers in a large zip-top plastic bag, squeeze out the air, and seal it closed. Smoosh the bag between your hands and the counter until the graham crackers are evenly crushed. Add your choice of berries to every cup, filling them a little less than halfway. Now add the Greek yogurt. Top with graham cracker crumbs and a drizzle of honey. Serve!

SECRET PUDDING

These delicious pudding cups are vegan and gluten-free, as well as keto-friendly. Enjoy!

MAKES 8 SERVINGS | PREP TIME: 30 MINUTES

whatcha need

5 avocados, halved and pitted

½ cup pure maple syrup

¼ teaspoon sea salt

¾ cup unsweetened cocoa powder

½ teaspoon vanilla extract

⅓ cup beverage-style coconut milk (I like vanilla)

Dark chocolate, for shaving

Edible flowers, for garnish

tools required

Large mixing bowl, whisk or hand mixer (optional), measuring cups/spoons, vegetable peeler, paring knife, serving bowls

whatcha gotta do

Scoop the avocado flesh into a bowl. Use a fork to soften the avocados and then stir in the maple syrup, sea salt, and cocoa powder. With your fork, mix them together well. Mix in the vanilla and coconut milk. Your ingredients should already look and feel like pudding. Now use a whisk to whip your mixture (a hand mixer is optional but will definitely make your life easier). The pudding should now be light and smooth.

Divide the pudding among dessert bowls or glasses. Use a vegetable peeler to shave chocolate over the tops of each serving of pudding and add an edible flower for garnish.

FRUIT CONES

What I love about this recipe is that it's quick and fast, kid-friendly . . . let's face it, these treats are everyone-friendly. They're a fun quick snack, and ice cream cones make the perfect bowls. Add some whipped cream and they look like real ice cream cones! Did I mention that you only have one item to clean, a spoon? Yes please!

MAKES AS MANY CONES AS YOUR PARTY REQUIRES (KEEP IN MIND YOU'LL BE USING ½ CUP OF FRUIT PER CONE) | PREP TIME: 10 MINUTES

whatcha need

Fruit of your choice

Ice cream cones (preferably flat-bottomed cones)

Powdered sugar, for sprinkling (optional)

Whipped cream (optional)

tools required

A spoon!

whatcha gotta do

First and foremost, rinse the fruit. Fill the cones with the fruit you have chosen and use your spoon to sprinkle your fruit with powdered sugar or top with a swirl of whipped cream.

POM NIBBLES

These bite-size desserts are pretty much effortless but they're absolutely delicious!

MAKES 24 TO 30 NIBBLES | PREP TIME: 8 MINUTES

whatcha need

30 thin wafer biscuits

1 (10-ounce) package goat cheese

1 (6-ounce) container pomegranate seeds

About 3 tablespoons honey

tools required

A spoon for honey, a butter knife, a pretty platter

whatcha gotta do

Gently spread goat cheese on each wafer and lay them out on your serving platter. Add a few pomegranate seeds to each and drizzle honey over.

COOKIE DOUGH BALLS

These bad boys will last you around five days in the fridge . . . but I doubt they'll stick around that long.

MAKES 24 BALLS | TOTAL TIME: 25 MINUTES

whatcha need

⅓ cup (about five tablespoons) unsalted butter, at room temperature

⅓ cup cane sugar

¼ teaspoon pink Himalayan sea salt

2 teaspoons vanilla extract

1 cup all-purpose flour, plus more if needed

½ cup chocolate chips (extra if you're feeling chocolaty)

tools required

Large mixing bowl, hand mixer, measuring cups/spoons, large zip-top plastic bag

whatcha gotta do

In a bowl, with a hand mixer, beat together the butter, sugar, salt, and vanilla extract. On low speed, slowly beat in the flour until all of the flour has been incorporated and your mixture resembles cookie dough. Now add the chocolate chips! I usually move to a spoon or clean hands from here. Once the chocolate chips are evenly distributed in the dough, roll the dough into 1-inch balls. Add them to the zip-top bag and freeze for 15 minutes to firm up. They are now ready to eat! If you're not ready to serve them, however, store them in the refrigerator for up to 5 days.

S'MORES COOKIES

These cookies are so yummy you're not gonna know what to do with yourself. For my sugar cookie recipe, turn to page 77.

MAKES 12 S'MORES COOKIES | TOTAL TIME: 60 MINUTES

whatcha need

CHEWIEST CHOCOLATE COOKIES:

1 stick (4 ounces) + 6 tablespoons unsalted butter

¾ cup dark brown sugar

½ cup cane sugar

2 teaspoons vanilla extract

1 teaspoon pink Himalayan sea salt

1 large egg

1 large egg yolk

1¾ cups all-purpose flour

½ teaspoon baking soda

1¼ cups chocolate chips

S'MORES TOPPING:

12 ounces large marshmallows

3 cups chocolate squares from baking bars (I like to use an assortment of flavors)

tools required

2 baking sheets, parchment paper, measuring cups/spoons, spatula, heatproof bowl, mixing bowls, whisk, cooling racks, medium saucepan, long skewers

whatcha gotta do

Preheat the oven to 375°F. Line the baking sheets with parchment paper.

In a saucepan, melt the butter over medium heat until it is golden brown but not burned, 1 to 2 minutes. Transfer the butter to a heatproof bowl and add both sugars. Whisk the butter and sugar mixture until evenly combined. Add the vanilla and salt and mix well. Add the whole egg and egg yolk and whisk until the mixture is smooth. Stir in the flour ¼ cup at a time. Mix in the baking soda until fluffy and with no lumps. Stir in the chocolate chips until they are distributed evenly throughout your dough. Refrigerate the dough for 30 minutes.

Roll the chilled dough into 1- to 2-inch balls and set a few inches apart on the lined baking sheets. Bake until the cookies are golden brown, 10 or so minutes. When the cookies are almost done, toast the marshmallows on skewers over the stove and set aside. Let the cookies cool on the pans on a cooling rack until they are pliable enough to lift off the parchment paper. Sandwich a chocolate square and a toasted marshmallow between two cookies and serve.

SUGAR COOKIE TARTS

MAKES 24 COOKIE TARTS | TOTAL TIME: 45 MINUTES

whatcha need

SUGAR COOKIES:

7 tablespoons unsalted butter

2¼ cups all-purpose flour

1 teaspoon baking powder

½ teaspoon baking soda

1½ cups + ⅓ cup cane sugar

1 large egg

4 tablespoons cream cheese

2 teaspoons vanilla extract

¼ teaspoon ground cinnamon

½ teaspoon sea salt

GLAZE:

2 cups powdered sugar

3 tablespoons whole milk

2 tablespoons cream cheese

ASSEMBLY:

3 cups fruit (I love raspberries, can you tell?)

tools required

2 baking sheets, mixing bowls, small saucepan, measuring cups/
spoons, parchment paper, spatula, whisk

whatcha gotta do

MAKE THE COOKIES: Preheat the oven to 350°F. Line the baking sheets with
parchment paper.

In a small saucepan, melt the butter over medium-low heat. In a medium bowl,
whisk together the flour, baking powder, and baking soda. In a second bowl,
combine 1½ cups of the sugar, the egg, cream cheese, vanilla extract, cinnamon,

and salt. Once the butter is melted, add it to the sugar and cream cheese mixture and whisk until smooth and free from lumps. Add the flour mixture ½ cup at a time. Mix until a dough texture has formed. Roll the dough into 1½- to 2-tablespoon balls and set 2 inches apart on the baking sheets. Bake until the cookies are just about reaching golden brown, 10 to 15 minutes. Let the cookies cool for a few minutes and then sprinkle the remaining ⅓ cup sugar over the tops of the cookies.

MAKE THE GLAZE: In a small bowl, whisk together the powdered sugar, milk, and cream cheese until smooth and free from lumps. Store in the refrigerator until ready to use. (The glaze can be refrigerated for up to 5 days.)

TO ASSEMBLE THE TARTS: Pour a teaspoon or so of the glaze delicately over each cookie and then top with fresh fruit. Ta-da!

DIRTY DIANA COOKIES

MAKES 24 COOKIES | TOTAL TIME: 60 MINUTES

whatcha need

1½ sticks (6 ounces) unsalted butter

⅓ cup dark brown sugar

1½ cups cane sugar

1½ teaspoons vanilla extract

1 large egg white

2 cups all-purpose flour

¾ cup unsweetened cocoa powder

1 teaspoon baking soda

¼ teaspoon sea salt

4 ounces dark chocolate

2 cups milk chocolate chunks

tools required

Stand mixer with a paddle attachment or hand mixer, mixing bowls, measuring cups/spoons, spatula, double boiler, 2 baking sheets, parchment paper, cooling rack, whisk

whatcha gotta do

In a bowl, with a mixer (use the paddle attachment if a stand mixer), beat together the butter, brown sugar, and cane sugar until light and fluffy. Beat in the vanilla and egg white. In a separate bowl, whisk together the flour, cocoa, baking soda, and sea salt.

In a double boiler, melt the dark chocolate. Let cool for 2 minutes, then beat into the butter-sugar mixture. On low speed, beat in the flour mixture ½ cup at a time. Add in the chocolate chunks. Once the mixture is dough-like, refrigerate for 30 minutes.

Preheat the oven to 375°F. Line the baking sheets with parchment paper.

Roll the cookie dough into 2-tablespoon balls, place on the lined baking sheets, and smoosh slightly. Bake for 10 to 12 minutes, until the cookies start to become shiny with some little "cracks" on top. Pull out of the oven right before they are fully cooked. Let them cool on cooling racks for 5 minutes or so before serving.

tip Add some chili powder for a kick!

ADULT COOKIES AND MILK

MAKES 8 SERVINGS | PREP TIME: 1½ HOURS

whatcha need

Chewiest Chocolate Cookies (from S'mores Cookies, page 74)

ADULT MILK:

1 cup long-grain rice

4 cups unsweetened beverage-style coconut milk

½ cup condensed milk

⅓ cup sugar

2 teaspoons vanilla extract

2 teaspoons ground cinnamon

¼ teaspoon ground cloves

8 to 10 ounces dark rum, to taste

tools required

2 large bowls, large pitcher, food processor (or high-powered blender), strainer

whatcha gotta do

Bake the chocolate cookies, but omit the s'mores topping.

MAKE THE ADULT MILK: In a large bowl, soak the rice in 2 cups water for 1 hour. Once the hour is complete, drain the rice. In a food processor (or high-powered blender), combine the rice and 2 cups of the coconut milk and process on high until fully combined and pureed. Strain the rice milk mixture into a large bowl. Rinse out the food processor. Return the strained rice milk to the food processor and add the remaining 2 cups coconut milk, the condensed milk, sugar, vanilla, cinnamon, cloves, and rum and mix on high for 2 minutes. Strain the spiked milk into a serving pitcher and serve with cookies (or drink by itself).

tip This adult milk recipe is delicious hot, too!

BANANA BREAD

whatcha need

Oil, for the pans

3 large or 4 small overripe bananas

2 sticks (8 ounces) unsalted butter, at room temperature

1 cup cane sugar

2 large eggs

2 tablespoons honey

1 teaspoon vanilla extract

2 cups all-purpose flour

1 teaspoon baking soda

1 teaspoon ground cinnamon

¾ teaspoon sea salt

½ teaspoon ground nutmeg

tools required

12 mini loaf pans or 2 regular loaf pans, mixing bowl, hand mixer, measuring cups/spoons, spatula

whatcha gotta do

Preheat the oven to 375°F. Grease 12 mini loaf pans (or 2 regular loaf pans) with oil.

In a bowl, with a hand mixer, beat the bananas, softened butter, and sugar together until combined well. Add the eggs, honey, and vanilla. Slowly mix in the flour, then beat in the baking soda, cinnamon, salt, and nutmeg. Fill each loaf pan halfway with batter.

Bake until golden brown, about 15 minutes. If you are using a regular loaf pan, plan for an extra 5 minutes of baking time. You want the banana breads to be soft, so make sure you don't overcook them. Let them cool for 15 minutes in their pans before serving.

tip It's best to serve banana bread fresh and warm with butter.

SWEET

85

WHISKEY CUPCAKES

MAKES 24 CUPCAKES | PREP TIME: 35 MINUTES

whatcha need

CUPCAKES:

3 cups all-purpose flour

2 teaspoons baking powder

¼ teaspoon ground cinnamon

¾ teaspoon sea salt

2 sticks (8 ounces) unsalted butter, at room temperature

1½ cups cane sugar

4 large eggs

1 large egg white

1½ cups whole milk

1 tablespoon whiskey

1 teaspoon vanilla extract

FROSTING:

2½ sticks (10 ounces) unsalted butter, at room temperature

1 cup powdered sugar

1 cup unsweetened cocoa powder

¼ teaspoon ground cinnamon

Pinch of sea salt

¾ cup honey

½ teaspoon whiskey

½ teaspoon vanilla extract

tools required

Stand mixer with a paddle attachment, hand mixer, 2 muffin tins, cupcake liners, mixing bowls, measuring cups/spoons, whisk, spatula, cooling racks, piping bag with a medium tip or a zip-top plastic bag with about 2 centimeters snipped off of one bottom corner

whatcha gotta do

MAKE THE CUPCAKES: Preheat the oven to 350°F. Line 24 cups of 2 muffin tins with paper liners.

In a bowl, whisk together the flour, baking powder, cinnamon, and sea salt. In a stand mixer with the paddle attachment, beat the butter, cane sugar, whole eggs, and egg white on medium speed until fluffy. Beat in the milk, whiskey, and vanilla slowly on low until fluffy and combined. Spoon 1½ to 2 tablespoons of cupcake batter into each muffin cup.

Bake until the cupcakes are golden brown and fully baked, 25 to 30 minutes. Check by inserting a toothpick into a cupcake. If it comes out without batter, they're ready. Gently remove the cupcakes from the muffin tins and let them rest on cooling racks for 1 hour.

MAKE THE FROSTING: In a bowl, with a hand mixer, beat together the butter, powdered sugar, cocoa, cinnamon, and sea salt until fully combined. Beat in the honey, whiskey, and vanilla until fluffy and completely combined. Refrigerate until ready to use.

When the cupcakes have cooled and are ready to be frosted, add the frosting to a piping bag fitted with a medium plain tip. Slowly work your way from the edge to the middle of the cupcakes. Make sure you apply medium pressure to the piping bag consistently for an even frosting application. Serve!

HOMEMADE BISCUITS

whatcha need

2 cups all-purpose flour, plus more for rolling out

1 teaspoon baking powder

1 teaspoon sea salt

¾ cup chilled buttermilk

2 sticks (8 ounces) unsalted butter, at room temperature,
+ 2 tablespoons melted

Jam (especially raspberry), for serving

Clotted cream, for serving

tools required

2 baking sheets, stand mixer, large mixing bowl, rolling pin, 2-inch
biscuit cutter, measuring cups/spoons, parchment paper, whisk

whatcha gotta do

Preheat the oven to 475°F. Line the baking sheets with parchment paper.

In a bowl, whisk together the flour, baking powder, and sea salt. Slowly add the flour mixture and buttermilk into the bowl of a stand mixer and mix. Add the softened butter and the melted butter to the mixer and beat until fully combined and a dough has formed. Turn the dough out onto a lightly floured surface. Knead the dough a few times and then roll it out until the dough is ¾ inch thick and smooth. Use a 2-inch biscuit cutter to cut out the dough and set the rounds on the prepared baking sheets about 1½ inches apart.

Bake until the biscuits are golden brown and hold their shape well, about 10 minutes. Serve warm with jam and clotted cream!

VANILLA LOVERS' CAKE

This cake is so great for beginners, or those at any experience level, because it combines time efficiency, simplicity, and style.

MAKES 6 TO 8 SERVINGS | TOTAL TIME: 3 HOURS

whatcha need

CAKE:

2 sticks (8 ounces) unsalted butter, at room temperature, plus more for the pans

3 cups all-purpose flour

2 teaspoons baking powder

½ teaspoon sea salt

½ teaspoon ground cinnamon

1¼ cups cane sugar

1 tablespoon vanilla extract

4 large eggs

1½ cups whole milk

⅓ cup condensed milk

FROSTING:

6 large egg yolks

¾ cup cane sugar

½ cup honey

4 sticks (1 pound) unsalted butter, at room temperature

2½ teaspoons vanilla extract

¼ teaspoon sea salt

Natural food coloring (optional)

Powdered sugar, for sprinkling

Flowers, for garnish

tools required

Stand mixer with a paddle attachment, hand mixer, mixing bowls, spatula, measuring cups/spoons, two 9-inch cake pans, cooling racks, parchment paper, piping bag, icing spatula, small pot

*there's nothing
a cake can't solve.*

whatcha gotta do

MAKE THE CAKE: Preheat the oven to 375°F. Place two 9-inch cake pans on a sheet of parchment paper and trace around them to make two circles. Cut out the two parchment paper rounds. Grease insides of the cake pans with butter and then add the parchment paper rounds.

In a bowl, mix together the flour, baking powder, sea salt, and cinnamon. In a stand mixer with the paddle attachment, beat the butter and sugar until fluffy. Beat in the vanilla and eggs one at a time, then add the milk and condensed milk. Beat in the flour mixture slowly on medium speed until the batter has no air bubbles or flour pockets.

Divide the batter between the cake pans. Bake until golden brown and cooked through the middle, about 30 minutes. Let cool in the pans for 1 hour, then gently turn the cakes out of their pans and set on the cooling racks for 1 hour more.

MAKE THE FROSTING: In a bowl, with a mixer, whisk the egg yolks on medium speed. In a small pot, bring the sugar and honey to a boil, stirring until fully dissolved. With the mixer running, slowly and evenly add the mixture to the egg yolks and whip on high until fluffy, about 8 minutes. Reduce the speed on the mixer and beat in the butter, vanilla, and sea salt. Whip on medium-high speed until the mixture is completely combined. (If you want your frosting to be a certain color, add food coloring in now.) Whip until the buttercream is smooth. Add the buttercream to a piping bag fitted with a medium round tip. Refrigerate if frosting gets warm.

Lay your first cake layer on parchment paper so it's easy to move later. With the piping bag, slowly pipe around the top of the first layer, applying medium pressure and a generous amount of frosting. Gently place the second layer evenly over the first and repeat the same frosting process. Use an icing spatula to gently smooth the frosting over the top of the cake. Sprinkle powdered sugar over the top and add any extra decorations as desired.

tip 1 I love adding edible flowers to my desserts; it creates a professional look with little effort. But make sure to remove all flowers and foliage—like the eucalyptus leaves I've used, which are toxic if ingested—before serving.

tip 2 You can slice each cake layer horizontally in half by gently sawing with a bread knife. Make sure you cut the cake evenly as to not look lopsided. By cutting the layers in half and applying the same frosting process above, you will create a four-layer cake, adding extra flair to your masterpiece.

SWEET

COBBLER À LA MODE

I love this recipe because it's easy, delicious, and virtually impossible to mess up!

MAKES 6 TO 8 SERVINGS | PREP TIME: 35 MINUTES

whatcha need

Coconut oil, for the baking dish

8 peaches, peeled, pitted, and cut into medium chunks

¼ cup cane sugar

½ cup + 2 tablespoons all-purpose flour

2 tablespoons whole milk

⅔ cup dark brown sugar

½ teaspoon baking powder

1 teaspoon ground cinnamon

¼ teaspoon ground nutmeg

Sea salt

⅓ cup unsalted butter, at room temperature

1 teaspoon fresh lemon juice

½ teaspoon vanilla extract

Vanilla bean ice cream, for serving

tools required

Hand mixer, mixing bowls, chef's knife, 4-quart baking dish, measuring cups/spoons

whatcha gotta do

Preheat the oven to 375°F. Grease a 4-quart baking dish with coconut oil.

In a large bowl, toss the peaches with the cane sugar and set aside. In a separate bowl, with a hand mixer, combine ½ cup of the flour, the milk, brown sugar, baking powder, cinnamon, nutmeg, pinch of sea salt, and the butter. Refrigerate the topping mixture until you're ready to use it.

To the bowl of peaches, add the remaining 2 tablespoons flour, lemon juice, vanilla, and another pinch of sea salt. Combine the ingredients well.

Scrape the peaches into the baking dish. Cover with the topping mixture. Bake until golden brown, 30 or so minutes.

Serve the cobbler in individual bowls with a scoop of vanilla bean ice cream.

SIPS

polite

sassy

virgin

POMEGRANATE PARADISE

This drink can fit so many occasions! Visit pages 182-183 to see how I use it for Halloween.

MAKES 1 COCKTAIL

whatcha need

Ice

3 ounces pomegranate juice

2 ounces ruby red grapefruit juice

1½ ounces vodka

Splash of fresh lime juice

Garnish (I like to use dehydrated grapefruit)

tools required

Large cocktail shaker with strainer, martini glass

whatcha gotta do

In a cocktail shaker one-quarter filled with ice, combine the pomegranate juice, grapefruit juice, vodka, and lime juice. Shake well and strain into a martini glass. Garnish and serve.

psst This drink tastes great without vodka, too!

ELDERFLOWER MULE

This drink is by far my favorite! It's so refreshing, and the elderflower liqueur gives it such a unique taste and twist on your regular mule.

MAKES 1 COCKTAIL

whatcha need

Ice

2 ounces tequila or vodka (I prefer tequila mules)

2 ounces elderflower liqueur

3 ounces ginger beer (not to be confused with ginger ale)

1 ounce club soda

½ ounce fresh lime juice

Fresh elderflower and other herbs, for garnish (optional but worth it)

tools required

Large cocktail shaker with strainer, classic copper mule mug or rocks glass

whatcha gotta do

In a cocktail shaker one-quarter filled with ice, combine the tequila, liqueur, ginger beer, club soda, and lime juice. Stir well and pour into an ice-filled mule mug or rocks glass. Garnish and serve.

LAVENDER ELECTRIC LEMONADE

SERVES 4 TO 8 DEPENDING ON WHO GOES BACK FOR SECONDS

whatcha need

2¼ cups lemonade

½ cup vodka

⅔ cup ginger beer

⅔ cup club soda

3 ounces lavender extract

4 lemons, thinly sliced

Ice

Lemon slices and lavender sprigs, for garnish (optional)

tools required

Large pitcher, long stirring spoon, serving glasses, paring knife

whatcha gotta do

In a large pitcher, combine the lemonade, vodka, ginger beer, club soda, and lavender extract and stir with a stirring spoon. Add the sliced lemons to the pitcher along with a few lavender sprigs. Add ice and give it another good stir. Garnishing the glasses with a lemon slice and lavender sprig is optional, but it gives your drinks that extra bit of class.

HUDSON'S MARTINI

I somewhat despise olives and vermouth, so this drink is truly Hudson's baby. He really enjoys a good martini, and by everyone else's response it's delicious. I love seeing how much he loves creating his own combinations, too.

MAKES 1 COCKTAIL

whatcha need

Dry vermouth "wash"

Ice

3 ounces vodka (your favorite)

Olive brine, to taste

Olives, for garnish

tools required

Cocktail shaker with strainer, martini glass, cocktail pick

whatcha gotta do

"Wash" a martini glass with vermouth: In other words, pour a small amount of vermouth into your glass, swish it around, and pour out the excess vermouth; you just want the vermouth to coat your glass, not fill it. We won't be needing that vermouth again, so feel free to pour it down the drain.

In a cocktail shaker one-quarter filled with ice, combine the vodka and olive brine (pour in a small amount first and add more if necessary). Shake well and strain into a martini glass. Spear some olives on a cocktail pick and use as garnish.

PINEAPPLE CHILE PEPPER BUBBLES

SERVES 6 TO 8

whatcha need

1 cup sugar

1 teaspoon chili powder

1½ cups pineapple juice (no sugar added)

1 pineapple

1 (750 ml) bottle champagne (your favorite)

Red pepper flakes, for garnish (optional)

tools required

Small saucepan, spatula, large pitcher, champagne flutes, small food container, stirring spoon, chef's knife, 1½-inch round cookie cutter

whatcha gotta do

In a small saucepan, heat the sugar, 1 cup water, and the chili powder over low heat, stirring occasionally. Once the sugar is dissolved, transfer the mixture to a small food storage container and refrigerate.

When the syrup is well chilled, transfer it to a pitcher and add the pineapple juice. Mix well and then refrigerate.

Meanwhile, with a sturdy chef's knife, cut the pineapple crosswise into ½-inch-thick slices. With a 1½-inch round cookie cutter, cut out shapes and slice a thin slit down one side. Set aside to use as garnish.

Pour champagne to come halfway up each glass, then top with the pineapple juice mixture. For an extra kick, add red pepper flakes to each glass. Set the pineapple cut-outs on the rims of the glasses and serve!

SPICY MANGO MARGARITA

SERVES 8

whatcha need

1 (34-ounce) bag frozen organic mango chunks

3 to 5 jalapeños, sliced, to taste

1 cup tequila (your favorite)

6 tablespoons + ¼ cup fresh lime juice

¼ cup pure maple syrup

1 cup ice

1 tablespoon Tajín Clasico

Tajín Clasico or sugar, for rimming glasses

Lime wheels, for garnish

tools required

Large pitcher, food processor, margarita glasses, paring knife,
rimmed plate, regular plate

whatcha gotta do

In a food processor, combine the mango chunks, jalapeños, tequila, 6 tablespoons
of the lime juice, 1½ cups water, the maple syrup, ice, and Tajín and puree on high
until completely smooth. Transfer to a pitcher.

On a rimmed plate, add the remaining ¼ cup lime juice. On a separate plate, add
a generous amount of either Tajín or sugar (whichever you prefer). Dip the rims of
margarita glasses in the lime juice and then coat in either Tajín or sugar. Garnish
each rimmed glass with a lime wheel. Pour in the margarita mixture and serve!

WHISKEY PEACH ICED TEA

whatcha need

1¾ cups peach nectar (no sugar added)

5 cups freshly brewed black tea, cooled

1 cup whiskey

5 tablespoons pure maple syrup

1 peach, sliced extra thin

Ice

Edible flowers and/or herbs, for garnish

tools required

Large pitcher, chef's knife, stirring spoon, rocks or coupe glasses

whatcha gotta do

Fill a large pitcher with the peach nectar, tea, whiskey, and maple syrup. Stir vigorously until fully combined and refrigerate until ready to serve. When ready to serve, pour whiskey tea into glasses filled with ice and garnish each glass with a peach slice, edible flowers, and/or herbs and serve!

SNEAKY SANGRIA

This sangria sneaks up on you, but it's oh so yummy!

whatcha need

2 (750 ml) bottles pinot noir

1 (750 ml) bottle sparkling wine

¾ cup elderflower liqueur

2 tablespoons triple sec

¼ cup orange juice (no sugar added)

¼ cup white grape or pear juice (no sugar added)

¼ cup apple juice (no sugar added)

3 cups strawberries, cut in half

4 oranges, sliced

2 cups grapes

Ice

tools required

Large pitcher or beverage dispenser, chef's knife, stirring spoon,
serving glasses

whatcha gotta do

In a 5-quart beverage dispenser, combine the wines, elderflower liqueur, triple sec, and all the fruit juices. Cover and refrigerate overnight. The day of serving, add sliced fruit and a generous amount of ice to the beverage container and stir. Serve!

KOOL KIWI

whatcha need

Ice

1 liter sparkling water

5 kiwis, peeled and sliced into rounds

3 tablespoons fresh lime juice

Stevia or agave nectar (optional)

Edible flowers, for garnish

tools required

Large pitcher, stirring spoon, paring knife, serving glasses

whatcha gotta do

In a large ice-filled pitcher, combine the sparkling water, kiwis, and lime juice. If you want a slightly sweeter option, add a few drops of stevia or 1 tablespoon agave nectar and stir. Once you've poured this yummy spa-like water into glasses, garnish with an edible flower.

LUSH LEMONADE

Lush Lemonade can easily be used for themed parties by adding natural food coloring. When a drink, like this lemonade, has a fairly neutral color it's easy to work into any theme.

SERVES 10 TO 14

whatcha need

2½ cups lemonade

1¼ cups pear juice (no sugar added)

1¼ cups peach juice (no sugar added)

2 cups water

3 tablespoons maple sugar

Natural food coloring (optional)

Ice

tools required

Extra-large pitcher or beverage dispenser, stirring spoon, serving glasses

whatcha gotta do

In a large pitcher, combine the lemonade, pear juice, peach juice, 2 cups water, maple sugar, and food coloring, if using. Stir well until all of the ingredients are combined. Refrigerate until ready to serve. Serve over ice.

STRAWBERRY LEMONADE WITH BASIL

whatcha need

6 cups strawberries, cut in half

2 cups lemonade

2 cups sparkling water

½ cup honey

2 cups ice

4 to 6 fresh basil leaves

tools required

Food processor, paring knife, serving glasses

whatcha gotta do

Set aside a few strawberries for garnish. In a food processor, combine the remaining strawberries, lemonade, sparkling water, honey, and ice and puree on high until completely smooth. Pour into serving glasses and garnish with a basil leaf and strawberry slices.

PARTY PREP

In my world, party prep is just as fun as the actual party. I love coming up with new ideas for entertaining guests, whether it's special recipes or themed DIY projects. Here is some food for thought to get you started . . .

WHAT'S THE OCCASION?

No matter the occasion, personalization is key. Whether that means spelling out the birthday boy or girl's name in big letters or adding my hubby's favorite cake to the dessert bar, I'll always find a way to their heart. Not sure where to start? I've listed a few questions to help you get those creative juices flowing, so grab a notepad and let's get started!

BIRTHDAY OR PERSONAL CELEBRATION

What's their favorite color?
What's their favorite food or drink?
What's their guilty pleasure?
What's their favorite activity or game?
What's their favorite place?
What's their favorite time of year?
Do they like to go out or stay home?
Do they like to stay up late or get up early?
Do they like surprises?

CELEBRATING TWO

Whether it's an engagement party or an anniversary, there are so many sweet ideas and fun ways to celebrate.

What's their favorite place to go together?
Where did they meet?
When did they meet?
Do they like to stay in or go out?
Do they have a favorite food or drink in common?
Do they have a favorite game or guilty pleasure in common?
Do they like surprises?

HOLIDAY OR ANNUAL CELEBRATION

Do you have any family traditions you want to include?
What do you absolutely have to have?
Do you want to celebrate inside or outside or both?
What color scheme do you want?

WHAT'S YOUR BUDGET?

Setting a party budget might not seem fun, but it's important to make a decision before you spend your money blindly. A budget gives you the boundaries you need to truly begin your party-planning process. In the past, I'd spend way too much money on parties, but at the end of the day my guests could care less about how

and unique. There are so many ways to save and make your budget go further, and no one will ever know the difference. With a few tips and tricks, you can make your party look expensive and classy. It's easy to get carried away with ideas and fantasies, so here's a chart (opposite) that shows you where to put your money regardless of whether your budget is $50 or $10,000.

No two parties are alike, and my budget chart is a loose example. You can alter it to emphasize what is most important to you, but be sure to plan within your means. Wanna know where to save? It's truly amazing what you can do yourself with a little imagination and some hot glue! Here are a few things to search for:

SALES: You can find some amazing decorations online or in your craft store sale sections.

FRESH FLOWERS AND FOLIAGE: You can do so much with greenery and some inexpensive vases.

FABRIC OR CURTAINS ON SALE: For a virtually free photo booth or tablecloth.

VINTAGE FINDS: From your local antique shop, these are the best for themed parties and they're great talking pieces!

much money I'd spent. Your friends and family appreciate the love and time you've put into your party more than the big expenses that you thought you needed to impress them. It's all about buying the right things, not the most expensive things, and the things that make your party feel personal

DECORATIONS	*50%*	Decorations are generally the most expensive party item and the most time-consuming to gather and put together. Whether I'm making my own or buying them, decorations take up a good chunk of my budget. They really set the mood for a party—whether it's small and intimate or a big gathering—and make your guests feel like they are in for an experience.
FOOD AND DRINKS	*40%*	There is no party without sipping and snacking! Designing a menu is so fun, especially when you have a theme to work with. There are plenty of yummy, crowd-pleasing foods you can make that won't break the bank! If you are in a rush and don't have time to make your own dishes, check out the Sammies (page 56) and the Grazing Table (page 59), two ideas for how you can have a stress-free party by letting your guests serve themselves. Don't be afraid to ask your guests to bring a drink or a dish, too—everyone loves a potluck!
ENTERTAINMENT	*5%*	You don't have to hire a popular boy band to perform at your house—although that would be cool—but you could plan for a game or activity that everyone can participate in. Whether it's a treasure hunt through the park, a costume contest, or board games, leave room in your party plan for some interactive fun.
INVITES	*5%*	Whichever way you choose to deliver your invitations, either by mail, phone, or email, they can be personal and beautiful! There are lots of cost-effective options. And you can always add fun details that let your guests know what kind of party it will be: Should they arrive in pajamas? Should they bring a bottle of wine? Personal touches and fun references truly make invitations inviting. We always list our home address as the "Hudsha Manor." One of our friends gave us that nickname and we've used it ever since.

You can save on food, too! If you're on a tight budget, choose more crowd-pleasing bite-size options! A well-thought-out grazing table will keep guests occupied and wowed for ages and will save you time and cash.

USE YOUR RESOURCES!

The Internet is an infinite fountain of ideas, so take advantage of it! Do you have a sense of what decorations or supplies you want but you don't know where to find them? Don't give up, ask Google! Search on eBay and Etsy and Amazon! You'll be glad you did. Online shopping also gives you the power to price check. Especially for those more expensive items, double-check if you can find them at a lower cost somewhere else. Visit your local hardware and dollar stores to find a lot of what you need for half the price of a regular party store. Utilize your friends and family by asking for help setting up or borrowing some décor! Not only is it fun to plan and prep with friends, but it also helps lower your stress level. Remember that everyone attending has the same goal—to have fun!

WHEN'S THE OCCASION?

If you're having trouble deciding when to have the party, consider checking the availability of the guests you know you absolutely want to be there. Once you've picked a day and time, you'll be able to plan your schedule. After that, everything else will fall into place. To be completely honest I've planned and executed a party within a few hours, so I promise it's possible!

I favor old-fashioned mail invites for letting your guests know when the occasion is, but that's not always possible. Thankfully, there are so many cute online invites that you can't go wrong! When you're designing your invites make sure they include details like this:

Date and time

Location and any necessary directions

RSVP by, to, and when

What to bring

Dress code

Adults-only or kids welcome

Inform of any food allergies

Any other helpful memos (for example, "Shhh, it's a surprise! Park around the corner!")

DO YOU WANT AN "ADULTS-ONLY" PARTY?

But you aren't sure how to ask your friends and family to get a sitter? It's easier than you think. Most of our friends have kiddos and the majority of the time we are absolutely thrilled to have them around! But every now and then we feel like it'll be safer and easier if the adults have a night out. Here's a couple of tips on how to approach it without any hurt feelings!

OPTION 1:
Put it on your invitations or send out the memo in a group text.

It never feels good to be singled out, so adding a "big kids only" label to your invite will gently tell your guests that they should enjoy a night out. If you want to be more casual about it, or only have a few friends with kids, add them to a group chat so that no one thinks you're pointing their kids out specifically.

OPTION 2:
Create a "kid zone."

We do this often and it works out great! If ruling out kids seems impractical for you and your guests, set up a kid zone in an area away from alcohol and breakables. Provide the kiddos with yummy parent-approved (allergy-cleared) snacks and some easy crafts and games to keep them occupied.

HOW MANY PEOPLE ARE YOU INVITING?

This is a question I am famous for because I tend to ignore it. I have learned my lesson the hard way. There have been multiple times when I've felt bad saying no to last-minute plus-ones (people whom I've never met) and sometimes it all works out perfectly . . . but other times it's disastrous. It's hard to say yes to some and no to others, so a good rule of thumb is to be consistent with your decision. It also depends on the kind of party you're throwing. If you're not serving a sit-down dinner, it's way easier! And if you know with plenty of time in advance, you can ask your guests to bring a bottle of wine or an appetizer to help out. Here are a few tips to help you avoid any unwanted mishaps.

ARE YOU ALLOWING PLUS-ONES?

Chances are if you don't specify, at least one person will bring a guest, which is no problem unless you're not ready for it (not enough food or drinks, etc.). If you're concerned about it, consider adding a "no plus-ones" note to your invite!

THE BIGGER THE PARTY THE BIGGER THE PRICE TAG

The more people that attend your party the higher the price tag, and the harder it is for you to stay on budget.

DO YOU HAVE ENOUGH SPACE?

Even if your budget is solid, keep in mind that your space might be the constraining factor. Make sure your space can accommodate all of the guests you want attending. If not, see if you can borrow someone else's space.

NAME TAGS

Using special touches like place cards and name tags can pose a challenge when you have surprise guests. To combat that concern, I always order extra blank tags or make them myself so I can fit in the last few if need be.

WHAT'S ON THE MENU?

The coolest thing about planning your menu around your party is that you can match your food to your theme. Check out page 176 to see how my rice crispy treats match our paint party. When you plan your menu, there are three questions you should ask yourself:

WHAT SEASON IS IT?

Depending on the time of year, you may not be able to get all of the ingredients you need for certain recipes, so keep seasonality in mind when deciding what to make.

IS YOUR MENU HEAD-COUNT FRIENDLY?

You may have too many guests to make some recipes cost-effective and efficient; choose things that scale easily and won't be too costly.

DO YOU HAVE ENOUGH VARIETY?

You want to make sure you have enough variety of salty, sweet, and healthy so that everyone can enjoy the grub!

WHAT SHOULD YOU DO?

- ☐ Have fun with your theme
- ☐ Create your budget
- ☐ Set a realistic party date
- ☐ Buy what you can ahead of time
- ☐ Be smart with your invite list
- ☐ Send out your invites in a timely fashion
- ☐ Decide on your menu based on season and price tag
- ☐ Make and put your decorations together ahead of time
- ☐ Buy perishable food and flowers the day of or the day before
- ☐ Make your party music playlist
- ☐ Let people help you
- ☐ Relax and have fun
- ☐ Accept that not everything will go your way and that's okay
- ☐ Let go. . . . Your guests won't know what you didn't have time for unless you tell them
- ☐ Remember to eat

HERE'S A COUPLE OF TIPS TO MAKE YOUR PARTY DAY GO SMOOTHER:

- ☐ Create a priority list and stick to it
- ☐ Cross off your "to do" list as you go—it truly makes you feel better
- ☐ Take a food break
- ☐ Get your friends to come over and help you in the morning
- ☐ Remember that most people arrive late anyway
- ☐ Remember that your guests just want to have fun and you should too
- ☐ Breathe and smile
- ☐ Remember that a 2 a.m. pizza delivery doesn't mean you didn't have enough food, it means your guests love your company

ARE YOU THROWING A PARTY THAT YOU KNOW IS GONNA GO PRETTY LATE?

You might want to be prepared for a few guests to sleep over. A lot of our friends and family come from out of town or hours away and we often invite them to stay the night (especially if we've been serving alcohol as part of the party menu). You don't have to have fancy guest rooms to make your guests feel comfortable, just a few toiletries and conveniences. If your guests prefer to head home at night, and are able to do so, don't forget to send them home with coffee as a little treat and a safe way to keep them alert after a fun night together.

There are a few essentials that matter to everyone, and all you need is the travel section in a convenience store to make your guests feel comfortable.

Sleepover-size necessities:

Toothbrush

Deodorant

Floss

Contact solution

Shampoo and conditioner

Body wash

WINDING DOWN THE PARTY

Everyone likes to have fun at a party, and it's important to take good care of yourself after you do! Socializing and eating and drinking can be so fun but so exhausting, so whether our guests are staying the night or safely heading home, we love to play a round of water pong to wind down the evening. The game is set up exactly like beer pong but revolves around competitive H_2O drinking. I love that plastic cups come in so many cute and theme-worthy colors, so there's no excuse not to play a fun, responsible, and hydrating game.

QUICK PARTY TIPS

Having a summer block party? Save your guests by having bug spray and sunblock handy.

Speaking of summer . . . freeze some grapes and add them to your white wine or sangria to keep your drink nice and cold without watering it down!

Wanna make sure your Halloween party guests actually dress up? Have a costume contest for the best dressed and the best couple costumes! Winners get gift cards to fun local spots.

Easy party game: Looking for a way to keep kids (and adults) entertained? Buy some cheap trash cans and a couple of hula hoops . . . paint them to match your party theme . . . turn the trash cans upside down and space them a couple of feet apart and you've got a giant game of ring toss.

Fly problem? Cover your drinks with cupcake liners while you aren't sipping to keep them bug-free (but still cute)!

A wheelbarrow makes an amazing ice bucket!

Freeze flowers and water in ice molds to make your ice bucket fancy.

Make sure to have several trash cans conveniently located so your guests have no excuse for not throwing trash away.

Make sure to serve water with your other drinks so you and your guests stay hydrated.

IT'S ALL IN THE DETAILS

From the guest book to the party favors, the details matter! Here are a few creative ways to captivate your guests and make any party or intimate occasion you throw feel special and memorable!

PLACE CARDS AND TAGS

Tags come in handy for any party you may throw. I use them all the time to let guests know what ingredients I've used in the food or the drinks, allergy alerts, name tags for glasses, instructions for navigating the festivities, and so on.

For example, these cute drink tag initials (opposite, top left) are easy to make, budget friendly, and all you need are stickers, string, and tags from your local craft store. Even though they are super simple, the tags add a touch of elegance, and you can always make them a little flashier if you choose.

Whether you're hosting a sit-down dinner or any other kind of party, place cards keep things personal and they're a great solution for organizing tables. For example, it's a cute way to create a designated kids table or bring a seating chart to life. If you want to write a special note or a thank-you on your party favors, consider a personalized tag with a cute saying. I have so much fun creating tags like this "feeling chilly?" label (opposite, top right)—they instantly dress up blankets for a cozy fall party. The simplicity of debossed place cards effortlessly oozes class. Place cards are such a sweet detail; even if it's a small gathering, I still love to add that personal touch.

FLOWERS AND CANDLES

Is there anything more classic or more elevating than flowers and candles for decoration?

I love to place candles in clear vases (or old-fashioned candelabras) for an easy and inexpensive centerpiece. Citronella-infused tapers are especially great for outdoor dining and entertaining to keep unwanted bugs away. There's something about candles that fits perfectly into any aesthetic and really makes people feel like they're in for a special night.

Pairing candles with flowers in simple and unusual vases truly sets the tone for any party or get-together.

Flowers are another favorite accent of mine for party design. They're simple but effective—they look great, they're inviting, they smell wonderful, and they add a little touch of drama and color! Here are a few flower arrangement tips to keep your bouquets fresh and happy.

tip 1 Buy your flowers the day before or the day of if possible.

tip 2 Look for flowers that are partially or not quite yet blooming (you want them to open up on party day).

tip 3 Snip snip! Cut the leaves off the lower part of the stems for a polished look. Clip any dead petals and trim at least 1 inch from the bottom of the stems at an angle.

tip 4 Keep the flowers hydrated with plenty of water so they won't look wilted and droopy.

tip 5 Keep it chilly! Flowers should be kept in the coldest part of your home (the fridge is even better) so they look fresh for your party.

tip 6 Keep it clear! On party day, make sure you change out the water in the vase so your flowers stay healthy and the water isn't murky.

LETTERS AND NUMBERS

Using letters and numbers to decorate and personalize a party isn't just easy and cost-effective, it's also meaningful.

Prop letters and numbers can be used to spell out the name of a guest or the theme of the night or the milestone that you're celebrating to give the guests all of the feels. You can buy block letters and numbers, or even those you'd find at a hardware or craft store to decorate a mailbox or a front door, or you can print out or paint on numbers and letters and add them to wood or metal for a more personal touch. There are so many fun and affordable ways to make your party aesthetic come to life!

Crafting these details yourself gives you the freedom to make exactly what you want. Buying items that are already made can certainly be more convenient, but they're not always as affecting as something that comes from the heart.

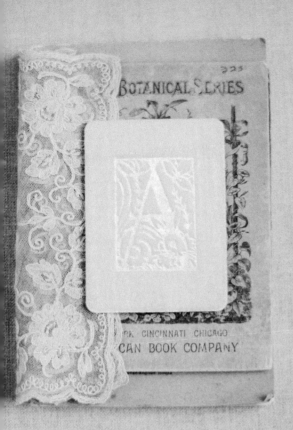

PHOTOS AND GUEST BOOKS

No matter how much work there is to do to pull everything together, I love capturing celebrations and making memories.

There's something so heartwarming about looking through photo albums from our parties and remembering all the fun memories that we created that night. In my opinion, the loveliest way to capture them is with a Polaroid camera. In our house, it's now a tradition that every party includes a Polaroid photo booth. But don't think that creating a photo booth is hard—all you need are some fun props, a camera, and a cute backdrop (curtains will do just fine).

I really like to include a guest book in the party vibe, too, as another way for guests to leave their mark on the event. For an example of an unconventional guest book from a kids paint party, see the photo opposite on the bottom left. I love how interactive and memorable this kind of guest book is. It can be kept forever and is as simple as 1, 2, 3. You just need some paint, friends, and a blank board or canvas.

A giant, towering guest book (opposite, top right) is another unique and interactive option. Every guest signs a block and piles their name up high, which makes for endless fun and sweet memories.

make sure to capture special moments.

PARTY FAVORS

Party favors have come a long way. There are so many thoughtful and practical gifts you can give as a nice thank-you to someone for taking the time to celebrate with you.

Guests always appreciate the gesture. And it never hurts if the favors are something enjoyable and useful. Mini sparkling wine bottles are so sweet (literally) and the label features a personalized thank-you note attached. You can get customized labels like these (opposite, top right) on Etsy or by purchasing an online template and printing them at home. Both are easy options that will impress your guests.

And there are plenty of other thoughtful ways to thank a guest for their company. Coasters and lavender bags are great favors for a housewarming party. Gorgeous stationery and sweet little books filled with poems are perfect for an engagement party. Dainty crowns are a lovely way to leave and remember a princess-themed birthday party. Little gifts like these can be found at craft stores, antique shops, and other gift stores, too.

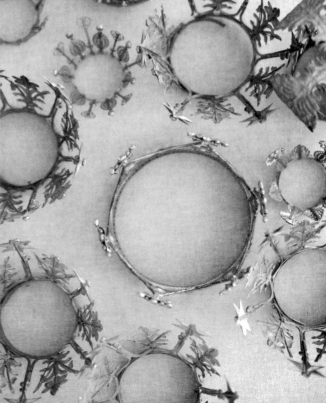

LET'S CELEBRATE

I hope that sharing some of my favorite ideas for parties and celebrations will inspire you to embark on your own creative journey. You can create an atmosphere that's beautiful and special for everyone, whether it's a quiet night at home, a dinner for two, a big family dinner, or a holiday celebration.

ROSES AND ROSÉ

You caught me pink-handed—this is one of my favorite ways to host.

This style works for brunch or nighttime, or, let's face it, any time. Dress this party up or down and it still has the same sense of class. A signature dessert and a signature cocktail make this party tasty and memorable. And this pink color palette has an effortless flow without being redundant. There can be a real harmony found in simplicity and this party is proof.

A Roses and Rosé theme can be used for a birthday party, a bachelorette party, a bridal shower, Sunday brunch, or even a baby shower. Adding two featured menu items elevates a party and allows you to play with an awesome display. I like to pair the Cotton Candy Cocktail (at right) with my tried and true Vanilla Lovers'

Cake (page 92). They're both sweet and their shades of pink are on point with this color scheme. Let me walk you through all the gorgeous and sweet things you'll need to make this dreamy idea possible. Don't forget to decorate with as many pink roses as your heart desires.

LEND ME SOME SUGAR
These yummy Cotton Candy Cocktails are simply magical.

1. Fill glasses with a generous amount of cotton candy.
2. When you're ready to sip, pour a rosé over the cotton candy and watch the magic happen.
3. Add some fresh berries to garnish.

got cake?
check out my vanilla
lovers' cake recipe
on page 92.

CIGAR BAR

Sometimes, my husband, Hudson, doesn't feel compelled to celebrate his birthday or doesn't have a clue what to do. So I came up with a foolproof idea that allows for a low-key celebration that still feels special and bonding for Hudson and his five brothers. Say hello to Cigar Night.

All you need is your love's favorite drink of choice and an assortment of their favorite cigars. (If people are particular, you can encourage guests to bring their own cigars.) What matters most here is the thought that you put into the night and the vibe you create. Think James Bond. We decided to have everyone dress up in suits and ties or fancy cocktail dresses. This style had everyone feeling classy and ready to have fun. We traded party music for jazz and we topped it off with a few poker tables, too. By the way, Hudson takes his martini shaken, not stirred.

VALENTINE'S DAY

I love *love.*

Valentine's Day was always hit or miss for me. It's three days before my birthday and it wasn't until I met Hudson that I started caring about it. We love to go on picnic dates for Valentine's and even though it's a simple thing to do, it's the company that matters, along with the tradition. Now, I welcome any excuse to celebrate love. And it isn't reserved for those with a significant other, either. I love celebrating my fur babies, my best friends, and my family.

A giant heart made entirely out of bite-size chocolates is a great example of how simple it is to get an "I love you" message across if you have loved ones over to celebrate.

SWEETHEART WAFFLES

How sweet are these? (Pun intended!) Serve these cut-out waffles with some maple syrup and powdered sugar, maybe some fruit and whipped cream . . . or whatever your heart desires (get it?). This is a cute idea for Valentine's Day breakfast, or a late-night meal with your special someone.

ANNIVERSARY

Sometimes all you need is a smile.

A party for two is just as good as a party for two hundred. One of the most beautiful parts of my relationship with my husband is how effortless our love is. We can spend absolutely every day together and never grow tired of one another (for the most part) and that is very rare and most definitely something to celebrate. Cheers to love that endures all things and is comfortable when dressed up, but more important, also when dressed down.

Surprise your better half with a toast of your appreciation.

Welcome your honey with some unexpected romantic words, or a list of the things you love most about them, and your favorite bubbly. Share a toast to the extraordinary feelings you share and how rare it is to find a home for your heart. A special homemade dinner and dessert is a lovely way to say thank you and share words, love, and what you are thankful for. If you only have a few minutes to spare, this gesture still goes a long way. After all, some of the most special memories of those we love happen in only a few moments.

FOR THE LOVE
OF FUR BABIES

Our dogs Lady and Levi are truly our babies. They have the biggest personalities and are simply the best. I couldn't imagine life without them.

For those of you who have puppy dog family members of your own, I'm excited to share this doggie birthday cake recipe. This is a great alternative to store-bought doggy baked goods that don't always have your pet's stomach in mind.

BIRTHDAY CAKE

This cake is dog-safe and packed with doggie probiotics, coat and skin nutrients, and sugar regulators (great for diabetic dogs). It's also irresistible for your pups, so it's a really delicious way to tell them you love them! If you're unsure about how the ingredients in this recipe will affect your special fur baby, always contact your vet first.

MAKES 2 SERVINGS—THIS RECIPE IS PERFECT FOR CELEBRATING TWO FUR BABIES OR FOR SAVING HALF FOR A TREAT THE NEXT DAY | PREP TIME: 15 MINUTES

whatcha need

3 tablespoons unrefined coconut oil, plus more for the pan

3 large eggs

1 teaspoon organic honey (nothing added)

2 tablespoons organic raw peanut butter (no salt added, canola oil–free)

2 cups coconut flour

Organic plain Greek yogurt, for icing

tools required

9-inch cake pan, mixing bowl, measuring cups/spoons, whisk, spatula

whatcha gotta do

Preheat the oven to 375°F. Oil a 9-inch cake pan with some coconut oil.

In a bowl, whisk together the eggs, 3 tablespoons coconut oil, the honey, and the peanut butter. Whisk in the coconut flour in stages until the batter is fully mixed with no clumps.

Pour the batter into the cake pan. Bake until lightly browned and baked through, about 20 minutes. Let cool and then gently remove the cake from its pan. Use the Greek yogurt to ice the cake and let your pups go at it!

EASTER

I've always liked Easter, but now that I have little nieces and nephews I absolutely love it!

My nieces and nephews love to paint and so do I, but I wanted to come up with a new spin on the usual Easter traditions. Instead of using real eggs (which spoil) and dye (which stains), I use wooden or découpage eggs.

ALL YOU NEED IS:

Water-based paint
The desired number of faux eggs
Paint brushes
Glitter
Stickers
Stencils
Any other decorating supplies you can think of

With supervision, a hot glue gun can take your eggs to the next level!

All you gotta do is paint your eggs, decorate them, and let them dry.

I prefer to fill my own Easter eggs with healthier candy and toys instead of buying the prepackaged kind. It does take more effort, but it's way better for you and the little ones.

Consider putting fun toys and crafts inside instead of candy, too!

SOME FILLER IDEAS INCLUDE:

Stickers
Necklaces and bracelets
Mini figurines
Coins
Healthy gummy bears

Another fun way to have an Easter egg hunt is to hide empty fake eggs with numbers on them (so you know that all have been found at the end). Prizes are awarded according to the number of eggs each person finds. It's a great way to avoid bad candy and melted chocolate altogether!

PAINT PARTY

Throwing a paint party is a great way to get everyone involved, from the little ones to the grown-ups to the grandparents. Here are some ideas and tips:

Ask everyone to bring their own canvas or you can provide them yourself. Plan on it being messy and make sure you have canvas drop cloths and aprons.

Water-based paints are always better for the cleanup later, especially if you have lots of little ones attending.

WHATCHA NEED

Paint and lots of it
Paintbrushes
Canvases
Tabletop easels
Protective cloths
Aprons

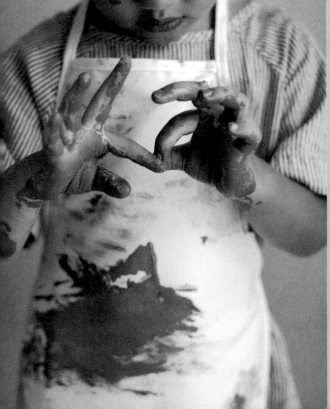

for favors: use mini paint cans and candy holders that kids can take home.

RICE CRISPY PAINT BRUSHES

MAKES 15 BRUSHES | PREP TIME: 60 MINUTES

whatcha need

4 tablespoons unsalted butter, plus more for the pan

7 cups marshmallows (the healthier the better)

1½ teaspoons vanilla extract

Pinch of sea salt

6¼ cups puffed rice cereal of your choosing (the healthier the better)

6 cups white melting chocolate

Natural food coloring (for desired "paint" color)

tools required

15 popsicle sticks, parchment paper, 9-inch square baking pan, spatula, medium saucepan, sharp knife, large mixing bowl

whatcha gotta do

Grease and line a 9-inch square baking pan with parchment paper. In a medium saucepan, melt the butter and marshmallows over medium heat until completely melted. Pour the mixture into a large bowl and stir in the vanilla and salt until evenly combined. Add the rice cereal and combine until evenly distributed. Scrape the rice cereal mixture into the lined baking pan and refrigerate until stiff, 15 to 20 minutes.

Meanwhile, in a clean saucepan, melt the chocolate over low heat until creamy. Stir in the food coloring.

When the rice cereal mixture is ready, slice it into rectangles. Remove the pieces from the baking pan and press a popsicle stick into the end of each. Then dip the rice crispy end into the melted white chocolate about halfway. Repeat with each popsicle, letting them dry on parchment paper. When the chocolate has completely hardened, serve!

WILD THING

The beauty of this party is that it's completely flexible for all age groups and gathering sizes.

Whether you're having a small family get-together or you have fifty kids running around, this setup works for both. Between the coziness of the tent and the undeniable comfort of s'mores . . . you can't go wrong, and it's fun for everyone. A little goes a long way.

Favors: These cute branch crayons and notepads cost me less than $30.

A little food coloring and some imagination can magically change a delicious lemonade (see Lush Lemonade, page 120) into a woodland drink!

Never lose your sparkle.

The best part about woodland whimsy is that everyone is invited.

HALLOWEEN

Hudson and I throw a Halloween party every year and now we have it down to an art. We've acquired a few staple décor pieces, including these miniature skeletons and creepy preserved specimens.

These blood bags are actually filled with something yummy . . . the ingredients for my Pomegranate Paradise cocktails! Go to page 103 to see how easily these cocktails fit into this theme.

You're never too old to beg for candy.

Witches
be crazy . . .

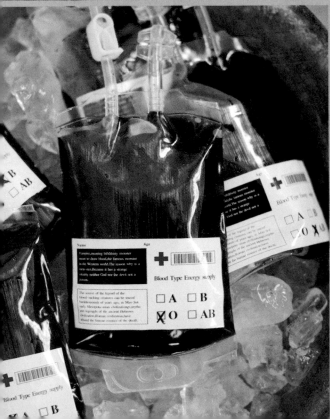

THANKFUL FOR THE SIMPLE THINGS . . .

I am thankful for so many things in my life, and I'm always extra thankful around Thanksgiving time.

We host an annual Friendsgiving and it's always the highlight of my year. Hudson and I are so blessed, especially in the friends and family department.

Break bread and cherish the ones you love.

Gobble 'til you wobble.

HARVEST CIDER

whatcha need

2 quarts apple juice (no sugar added)

2 cinnamon sticks

½ teaspoon ground cinnamon

1 tablespoon ground cloves

½ teaspoon ground nutmeg

½ teaspoon fresh lemon juice

2 oranges, thickly sliced

2 cups fresh cranberries

tools required

Large pot and lid, wooden spoon, chef's knife, measuring cups/spoons, heatproof glasses or mugs

whatcha gotta do

In a large pot, combine the apple juice, cinnamon sticks, ground cinnamon, cloves, nutmeg, and lemon juice and bring to a boil. Boil for 10 minutes and then reduce the heat to low. Add the orange slices and cranberries to the pot. Remove the cinnamon sticks and serve warm.

CHRISTMAS

Christmas is my absolute favorite time of year. I get so giddy that Hudson doesn't even know what to do with me! If I could start decorating for Christmas in August I would.

We didn't have a ton of holiday traditions when I was growing up, but there's one in particular that holds a special place in my heart. My mom saves little boxes from random things so she can use them to wrap presents that she arranges at our place settings for Christmas dinner.

I have taken on that tradition and I've also added a new one. I've always loved antique bells, and now I've started collecting them for Christmas. I've added some of them to cute mini trees and also to the Christmas presents on our table.

tip Tea boxes work really well for this little present!

fun fact There's an Irish wedding tradition where every guest gives the bride and groom a bell on their wedding day. At the end of their wedding, they string them all together. You're meant to ring the bells to remember your wedding vows. I just love that tradition, and it effortlessly matches with ours. Meant to be!

It's all fun and games
until Santa checks
the naughty list.

MAKE YOUR OWN ORNAMENTS

I love this craft because it's a craft the whole family can do together . . . and you'll actually want to show these ornaments off.

whatcha need

Clear plastic or glass ornaments

Dried or faux foliage

tools required

Scissors for cutting down to size

whatcha gotta do

Fill the ornaments with foliage and hang them on the tree or add them to a decorative bowl.

HOT COCOA

whatcha need

1 (4-ounce) dark chocolate baking bar

1 (8-ounce) package white chocolate chips

4 quarts whole milk

5 cups heavy cream

1 (14-ounce) can sweetened condensed milk

1 cup unsweetened cocoa powder

1 teaspoon vanilla extract

Mini marshmallows, for garnish (optional, but strongly encouraged)

tools required

Large pot with lid, double boiler, large heatproof beverage container, mugs for serving

whatcha gotta do

In a double boiler, melt the dark and white chocolate until smooth with no lumps.

Meanwhile, in a large pot, heat the milk, heavy cream, condensed milk, and cocoa powder over medium-high heat.

When the chocolate is completely melted, add it to the large pot and stir until the milk mixture and chocolate are completely combined. Stir in the vanilla extract.

When you're ready to serve the cocoa, transfer it to a heatproof beverage container and serve immediately. If desired, garnish with mini marshmallows.

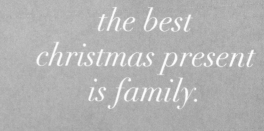

the best
christmas present
is family.

THANK YOU

I'm so glad that you took the time to explore *Sasha in Good Taste*.
I hope this book brings you joy and sparks your own journey
of cooking, party planning, and more. Remember to trust
your imagination and follow your vision. You are more powerful
than you know.

Love, Sasha

A QUICK BUT SPECIAL NOTE TO
MY FAMILY AND FRIENDS

Thank you for supporting me through this journey and for
believing in me even when I couldn't see the light at the end of
the tunnel. I am so proud of this accomplishment and I couldn't
have done it without each and every one of you. Also, to Lady and
Levi, who curled up next to me every day while I was writing . . .
Thank you for being patient and for snuggling with
me when I needed it most.

RESOURCES

Home décor and other items featured throughout
Sasha in Good Taste *can be found at the following places:*

www.casadeperrin.com

www.roughlinen.com

elsiegreen.com

www.unlikelyobjects.co

www.theartedepartment.com

INDEX

Page numbers in italics indicate photos

HarperCollins books may be purchased for educational, business, or sales promotional use. For information, please email the Special Markets Department at SPsales@harpercollins.com.

FIRST EDITION

Designed by Renata De Oliveira

Photographs by Elizabeth Messina

Library of Congress Cataloging-in-Publication Data has been applied for.

ISBN 978-0-06-285139-0

19 20 21 22 23   LSC   10 9 8 7 6 5 4 3 2 1